FROM HEAVEN TO EARTH:

WAGNER RETURNS

BY ROBERT R. LEICHTMAN, M.D.

The Twenty-First In A Series

ARIEL PRESS
THE PUBLISHING HOUSE OF LIGHT
COLUMBUS, OHIO

This book is made possible by gifts
to the Publications Fund of Light.

 Printed in the United States of America. Direct inquiries to: Ariel Press, 2557 Wickliffe Road, Columbus, Ohio 43221-1899. No royalties are paid on this book.

ISBN 0-89804-071-X

Library of Congress card catalog number: 82-72786

WAGNER RETURNS:

“Music is one of the great civilizing forces of humanity. It lifts us away from the animal state—far, far away—all the way to the sublime level of spirit. Music heals. Music soothes. It fills us with beauty and joy. In other words, *it makes us more than human.* Music—good music—must be considered as one of the ways God speaks to earth!”

“The majority of rock and roll music is disruptive and has a negative influence on people. It is violent music which churns the emotions of those listening to it to the point where they begin to have a physical response and behave in violent ways.”

“There is a crew of angels whose specific task is to maintain the quality of music on all levels. They are like the gardeners and supporters of music.”

“The person who strives to stand apart from the rest of humanity is going to be criticized just because he is, indeed, standing apart. The creative person must accept this and adjust to it—otherwise, he will not be able to function.”

“The dedication of the person who intends to write great music must approach a level of being intoxicated with the divine. For when he is, then inspiration pours forth and the composer is impelled to create with a majesty he could never summon through his personal resources.”

—Richard Wagner

A BRIEF INTRODUCTION

for the benefit of readers who are becoming acquainted with our series, From Heaven to Earth, *for the first time*

Wagner Returns is the twenty-first in a landmark series of books written by Dr. Robert Leichtman. Each book in this series is the transcript of a conversation, conducted mediumistically, between Dr. Leichtman and the spirit of a well-known leader or genius.

The interviews began in 1973. The first series of twelve, primarily with the spirits of outstanding psychics and mediums, was published during 1979 and 1980. The individuals interviewed in that series include the psychics Edgar Cayce, Arthur Ford, Eileen Garrett, and Stewart Edward White; the occultists C.W. Leadbeater, Helena P. Blavatsky, and Cheiro; the psychic investigator Sir Oliver Lodge; the psychologists Carl Jung and Sigmund Freud (in a joint interview); and William Shakespeare, Thomas Jefferson, and the electrical genius Nikola Tesla.

The popularity of the first series of interviews encouraged Dr. Leichtman to embark on a second set of twelve. This time, however, he decided to focus more specifically on the theme of bringing heaven to earth—not just in the sense of giving the spirits of highly intelligent and dedicated individuals another chance to be heard, but even more importantly, in the sense of showcasing the elements of an enlightened consciousness and how it acts on earth.

Toward that end, Dr. Leichtman composed a list of individuals he deemed to be *priests of God*—not conventional priests who lead religious rites in churches or temples, but agents of light who practice the presence of God in everything they do. These are priests of government, priests of art, priests of literature, priests of service, priests of finance and industry, priests of science, and priests of music. Their unifying characteristic is their capacity to find God in the midst of everyday life and, by the power, inspiration, and refinement of their talent and understanding, manifest something divine in their work. They are people who brought heaven to earth—in their lives—not just to worship and reveal it, *but to use it to transform the world!*

In addition to Richard Wagner, who surely qualifies as a priest of music, Dr. Leichtman chose to interview the following spirits:

Albert Schweitzer, as an example of enlightened service.

Rembrandt van Rijn, as a priest of the paintbrush.

Sir Winston Churchill, as a priest of leadership.

Paramahansa Yogananda, who brought the spiritual teachings of India to America, as a representative of the intelligent mystic.

Mark Twain, as a priest of the pen.

Albert Einstein, as an example of enlightened scientific inquiry.

Benjamin Franklin, as a representative of inspired diplomacy and brilliant philosophy.

Andrew Carnegie, who built a fortune in steel and then set a model for enlightened philanthropy.

Luther Burbank, as an example of the inspired steward of nature and God's creation.

Abraham Lincoln, who demonstrated the healing power of charity and patience during his Presidency.

The twelfth and final book in the second series will be an interview with a number of spirits: Alexander Hamilton, Thomas Jefferson, Benjamin Franklin, Franklin Delano Roosevelt, Harry Truman, Theodore Roosevelt, and George Washington. Called *The Destiny of America,* the interview discusses the nature of the American Spirit, the loss of economic freedom in America, bureaucracy, and the future of the United States.

As the title *From Heaven to Earth* suggests, the purpose of this project is to acquaint readers with the current thinking of these outstanding individuals, even though they have left their physical bodies and now work on the inner dimensions of reality. Many new ideas about government, art, service, civilization, and spiritual growth are set forth in the conversations—as well as a new revelation of the nature of the "priest of God." The interviews are not just academic discussions of the historical accomplishments of these people; they probe new frontiers of the human mind. Each is a thoughtful, witty, and lively exchange of ideas.

It is not the intent of this series to document the existence of life after death—or the effectiveness of mediumship in contacting the spirits of those who have left their physical bodies. Nor is it necessary, for these matters have been scientifically proven many times over in other writings—indeed, in many of the books written by the people interviewed in the first series. The doubting reader will find ample proof in the works of Sir Oliver Lodge, Stewart Edward White, Eileen Garrett, Madame Blavatsky, Arthur Ford, C.W. Leadbeater—and countless others.

Instead, the interviews in *From Heaven to Earth* are offered as a way of demonstrating that we need not be content with just an echo of great geniuses who have lived and died; their voices can literally be heard again. Their spirits and ideas can actually return to earth. Heaven is not some faraway place inaccessible to mortals. It can easily be contacted by competent psychics and mediums who have correctly trained themselves. And such contact can produce insight and new ideas of great importance.

A more complete introduction to the second series of interviews is contained in the book, Schweitzer Returns. *In it, the concept of the "priests of God" and the nature of these interviews is described in detail. A more complete introduction to the nature of intelligent mediumship and the origins of* From Heaven to Earth *can be found in the first book in the series,* Edgar Cayce Returns. *For information on ordering these books, or the entire series, please see page 104 in this volume.*

—Carl Japikse
ARIEL PRESS

WAGNER RETURNS

In many ways, Richard Wagner was a man of great contrasts. He almost single-handedly established the tradition of great German opera, and yet he had little use for the operatic tradition of his day. He scandalized Europe with his wild behavior, profligate spending, and incurable tendency to have affairs with married women—and yet he wrote some of the most sublime and spiritually-inspiring music known to man. He excited passions and controversy wherever he went. His opinions bordered on the edge of fanaticism. He was a strong man, and a weak man. He had almost no formal musical training, yet became one of the great musical innovators of the nineteenth century. He was a brilliant genius, and yet he was blind to some of the most blatant realities of life. If he had not been a composer of opera, he might well have been a remarkable subject for one!

Wagner (his name is pronounced Ree-card Vagner) wrote his first musical composition at the age of 20, in

1833, but he had a strong fascination with the theater as well as music. It was only natural, therefore, that his interests led him into opera. But the opera of his time was heavily burdened with set formulas and rigid traditions. When *Tannhauser* was first performed in Paris, for instance, it created an actual riot, because it did not include a ballet in the second act, as the tradition demanded!

The young composer, however, could not accept these limitations, and developed a lifestyle which challenged the assumptions society had made, not just in music and opera, but in every facet of living. He made bold declarations, joined in revolutions, languished in exile, and managed to stay one step ahead of the bill collectors most of the way.

The first half of his adult life was spent struggling for recognition, a would-be reformer who never quite got the chance to make the mark he sensed was his destiny. This was a time of frustration, disappointment, and depression for Wagner—but also a time when he refined his musical skills and developed his innovative approaches. It was likewise a time when he flirted with revolution and was forced into exile.

The second half of his career was no less hectic, but far more successful. In 1864, bankrupt and consigned by his musical contemporaries to oblivion (his operas demanded too much from them), he attracted the interest of young Louis II, who had just become king of Bavaria. The king gave Wagner funds, financed productions of his operas, and established his reputation.

The crowning glory of Wagner's career came with the construction of what he regarded a temple of culture and music, a permanent festival opera house in Bayreuth, Germany. It was here that the four operas in *The Ring of the Nibelungen* were first performed as a tetralogy in 1876, seven years before his death.

It would be easy to say that Wagner was unique, but then all innovative people are unusual. Because they dare to be different, they generally foment controversy and strong reactions. Because they resist their critics, and pursue their own sense of destiny, they are said to be rebellious. True innovation is never accomplished without a heavy price. One has to have a heroic vision and unfaltering commitment to pursue this kind of life. Few people have demonstrated this more dramatically than Richard Wagner.

There will undoubtedly be people who wonder why I chose to interview Wagner for this series—people who see him more as a highly flawed human being than a priest of anything. But these will be people who either do not understand Wagner and his music—or prefer not to understand him. To me, Wagner is a perfect example of the inspired musician—a musician who devoted his life to revealing the divine potential of music and showing that music could be used both to refine consciousness and heal the personality. His operas never fail to inspire me, to lift my thoughts and feelings above the mundane and into an inner world filled with beauty, joy, heroism, triumph, and glory. They show me the way to the soul, and recharge my personality with new vigor and enthusiasm for living. In many respects, in fact, his operas are each a carefully crafted lesson in one stage or another on the spiritual path. It is not possible to listen to them without being inspired, unless the listener is deaf. When a creative genius can command that kind of power and stimulate that kind of effect in his audience, all of the scandals, controversy, and fanaticism which may have attended his personal life become nothing but trivial details of minor historical importance.

While I am not a professional musician, and do not have any training in the technical niceties of music, I have appreciated the beauty and uplifting quality of good music since before I could count. My interest in Wagner and my questions in this interview reflect both this perspective and this limitation. Undoubtedly I overlooked asking some questions which might have fascinated more skilled inquisitors, and perhaps asked a few that may seem simple and uneducated. But I do not believe that this kind of interview is best used for asking technical questions anyway. I prefer to pursue a deeper understanding of the inner potential of the genius which motivated the subjects I choose.

In my own investigations, I have found music to be an ideal avenue for exploring the phenomena of the fourth dimension and the intangible qualities within form. Like other major aspects of life, music has an outer form and an inner spirit. Part of music is tangible and audible, part of it intangible and inaudible. Part of the effect of music is obvious, part of it subtle. In fact, music has a capacity to speak directly to our unconscious and subconscious minds. It is therefore an extremely powerful medium.

In Wagner, I find a musician who not only recognized this inner reality of music but also explored it fearlessly. The movement of action in his operas is not so much the movement of a plot as it is the movement of psychological motivations. From his work we derived the term *leitmotif*, meaning "leading motive."

He was fascinated by the study of what drove people onward, especially at the mythological and cultural level.

Not surprisingly, this inner richness of music became one of the major topics of conversation in the interview that follows. Wagner boldly labels music as one of the languages of God, and proceeds to explain that good music can build and heal, while other music can destroy and harm.

This is a point of view I was delighted to hear. To my way of thinking, music such as Wagner's can stimulate aspiration, idealism, a sense of nobility, an awareness of heroic struggle, awe for the grandeur of the divine, and a respect for sacrifice, grace in defeat, and meaning in tragedy. It can reveal God. Destructive music, on the other hand, can stir up rebellious and hedonistic emotions, anger, and other harmful urges and attitudes. It can be quite harmful to the mind and the emotions.

Wagner explores this difference in music at great length. The ideas that Wagner presents—not from the perspective of the personality he worked through one hundred years ago, but from his current perspective on the inner planes—may seem controversial, opinionated, and challenging to some readers, but they are presented in the hope of arousing the discerning reader to look for the evidence of these issues for himself or herself. There is no question that music is much more than mere sound, mere entertainment. And it is important that we become aware of the inner side of music and its effects on us, so that we can learn, as Wagner warns, to filter out some of the more harmful types.

Wagner also discusses the creative process itself,

both as he experienced it in physical life and as he views it now from his current perspective. What was then a mysterious and mostly automatic process of his unconscious mind is now a subject he can—and does—discuss lucidly. He comments at length on the many problems which the highly creative person must face—fluctuating energy levels, fits of despair and elation, and intense criticism from others. He confesses that the fine point of the creative focus can easily blind a person to the creative work and style of others—and distort one's own perspective about the importance of the work he is doing. In all, Wagner presents one of the most brilliant commentaries on the problems of creative people that I have ever heard. Giving birth to "thought-children" seems to be no less stressful—or exciting—than giving birth to physical babies.

Naturally, we also talk at length about the enlightened way to listen to music and appreciate it in its fullest depth. I was consistently impressed by how deeply Wagner loves music, and how strongly he seeks to convey this love and reverence to others. His comments will be helpful to anyone who considers music to be a valuable part of his or her life, and may perhaps awaken a new interest in music in others.

Throughout, I was struck by the candor with which Wagner spoke. He was not reluctant, for example, to talk about the recent attempts of some people and groups to link him with Hitler—in fact he welcomed the chance to show how ridiculous it was to blame him for the actions of someone who did not rise to power until fifty years after Wagner's death! He also talked frankly about his personal weaknesses, his fanaticism, and his excesses. In all, it is a fascinating discussion.

It is with some pleasure that I note that this book is being issued during the centennial anniversary of Wagner's death, in 1883. If anyone who reads this interview is not familiar with his operas, I would highly recommend making it a point to attend a performance of at least one of them or, failing that, to listen to one of the excellent recordings of them now available. I especially recommend *Parsifal, The Meistersingers, Lohengrin,* and the four operas in *The Ring of the Nibelungen*.

The medium for this interview was my good friend David Kendrick Johnson. I am joined in asking questions by my friend and colleague Carl Japikse.

Wagner: You know, this is actually quite comfortable.

Leichtman: We aim to please. *[Laughter.]*

Wagner: I don't have an opening statement, so I will rely on you to get the conversation started.

Leichtman: All right. My first question is quite general. In your life as Richard Wagner, you stated that opera was the greatest of all art forms, and that the other arts should be seen as secondary to music. Has your view on this issue changed at all?

Wagner [chuckling]: A good many people were upset by that proclamation, as you might expect. In fact, as I recall it, they were more than upset.

That is the sort of opinion which comes back to haunt you in later life—and the after life, for that matter—but I hope you understand that I was viewing my work from the inside out. I was intensely involved in the act of creating music and opera, and this gave me an entirely different perspective than an outside observer would have. I fell into a kind of intense chauvinism toward my work and the whole genre or art form in which I was working.

This tends to happen to many artists and other innovative people who lead their field into new territory. The comment must be seen in this context.

It will be no surprise to you, I'm sure, that yes, I have changed my point of view. I regard opera as a synthesis of music and sculpture, dance, color, and gracefulness. It has a third- and fourth-dimensional quality which is sometimes missing in other art forms. But opera is just one of many excellent art forms, all of which must be ranked as valuable facets of civilization.

Leichtman: I'm sure Rembrandt, Shakespeare, and Mark Twain are relieved to hear you admit that.

[Laughter.]

Wagner: Opera and the theater have, perhaps, a more direct impact on the intellect than some other art forms do, but in no way can I honestly claim that the rest of the arts should be subservient to opera.

Actually, now that I have a bit broader perspective than I enjoyed before, I can see that the creative process is remarkably similar in all of the arts. In comparing notes with Rembrandt, for instance, I have discovered that he experienced the same quality of consciousness when he was painting that I registered when I was composing, conducting, and listening to music. I used to think of it as the musical essence of the creative inspiration itself. It was a bit intoxicating. Good painters and writers would think of it as the artistic essence or the literary essence—if they bothered to give it a label at all. But it really is the essence or enthusiasm generated by the creative process itself, and it is the same for all types of creative endeavor.

Japikse: A mixture of joy, insight, beauty, and the spark of creativity.

Wagner: Yes, it can be very intoxicating.

Leichtman: So that even though the art form may vary, the subjective interaction of the artist with his creative impulse will often be similar.

Wagner: Exactly. And this was the root of my musical chauvinism. Because I had a strong musical feeling at every stage of the creative process, and thought in terms of music, I made the assumption that music was the essence of all creativity. Now I see that this is too narrow a view. The artist might just as easily say that beauty is the essence of all creativity.

Leichtman: There are some people who claim that angels participate more in the creative inspiration of music than in other art forms. Is this true?

Wagner: I don't think I can accept that. Angels may well be present whenever any innovative genius is creating something outstanding. It's not limited to music.

Leichtman: Would the creative person be able to see the angelic forces and consciously respond to them?

Wagner: The extent of the awareness would be different for each individual. An artist would actually be more likely to see angels than a musician or a writer, because artists are usually more visually oriented. But seeing angels is not a necessary part of the creative process. For many creative geniuses, there is simply an awareness that something outstanding—something holy—is present and inspiring them. It is usually very subtle—a deepening of the respect the genius has for the work he is doing almost to a level of reverence and awe.

Please understand that most creative people do not bother to translate the subtle feelings they experience while working into words, as I am doing now. They just know that their state of mind and emotion is quite different during the act of creation than it ordinarily is—and that many of their peak experiences occur at this level of consciousness.

Leichtman: From reading about you, I have gathered that whole musical themes would simply well up within your awareness, and you would have to write at a frenzied pace to get it all down on paper before the inspiration escaped. Was that how you experienced angelic inspiration?

Wagner: Yes, that is correct. That level of creative inspiration is really a spiritual frenzy—the kind of passion a person in a peak state of devotion and religious awe would feel.

Leichtman: It sounds as though this sort of experience could be quite exhausting.

Wagner: It was, but as long as the strong surge of inspiration was there, it impelled me through long and extremely productive periods of creativity. But after the surge had subsided, it would be followed by an inevitable letdown. Many creative people go through this kind of cycle.

Unfortunately, I didn't understand the cycle very well during my physical lifetime. I interpreted the period which followed the surge to be a low energy period, and became rather frustrated and irritable—even sick. Now I understand that the body and mind simply need rest after a burst of creative work. I should have accepted the cycle for what it was and used it to rest up and pursue more tranquil activities.

Now, I don't mean to imply that all creative people experience the same intense peaks and valleys of emotion and vitality that I did. Other people have different styles. But this instability of energy, focus, and mood is something most creative people have to cope with. I didn't handle the problem well in my lifetime—and I certainly wouldn't want other people looking at the way I handled it and think I set a good example. I didn't.

Leichtman: You are even noted for having suffered a great deal from depression during those periods of low energy.

Wagner: When you can't get the work done, when you can't bring the inspiration through, you can become very depressed. It is difficult to endure.

Leichtman: It would seem that artistic people have a greater need than the average person to learn about the process of self-renewal.

Wagner: I would agree. I can remember being depressed for days and days and days early in my life. It seemed the depression would never go away, but eventually I learned to work around it. I would get out and take walks, or visit with people, or engage myself in similar activities which would break the depression.

Leichtman: Did you learn to pace yourself better?

Wagner: Pacing yourself is not always possible, unfortunately, because it is frequently the inspiration which determines the pace of your work, not a predetermined, reasonable schedule. When the inspiration starts pouring in, you have to go with the tide. And when the tide runs out, you have to learn to do other things.

Leichtman: I had the impression from reading about

you that you periodically experienced bouts of what we might call "the dark night of the soul." Your inspiration would lift you up to lofty heights where you felt in touch with the universe and its ideals, only to be thrown back down to earth and its gloom. This apparently was very discouraging to you.

Wagner: Yes. As you have suggested, the creative person often does hit peaks of experience in his work, and once you have hit the peak, the simple act of returning to mundane living can be depressing by comparison. Daily life just doesn't seem very important in contrast—it seems banal and boring. Of course, that is something of an illusion, and you have to learn to pull yourself through these periods.

Leichtman: What would you recommend to creative people who do experience rather marked swings of peak energy and productivity followed by very low periods of depression or boredom?

Wagner: I can only suggest a few general ideas that might have worked for me. Keep in mind that the truly creative person is often highly individualistic, and what might have worked for me, if I had tried it, might not work for someone else.

I suppose the first thing this type of person should do is accept the fact that his energy and creative output are going to vary from day to day, and so he must learn not to get so upset when every day does not measure up to his standards of peak performance and feeling. The problem for many creative people is often one of their own making. They allow their frustration and irritability to build up, and this adds to their exhaustion. And so they must accept the fact that the creative apparatus of the mind occasionally needs rest—it can't work at high levels all the time any more than the physical body can perform hard physical labor sixteen hours a day.

Creative people must learn to accept the need for rest and self-renewal gracefully. But this is part of the problem. Highly creative people are often bored when they are not busily communing with their muse. This is a great mistake. They need to involve themselves in other worthwhile pursuits to take up the slack. These other activities can be creative as well, but they need to be of a different type than their primary activity and love.

Japikse: Some of your biographies indicate that you studied Oriental religions—Buddhism for one. Did you find these philosophies helpful to you in your work—or in life in general?

Wagner: I did not practice an Eastern type of meditation, but some of the ideas were useful, yes. They helped me understand more of the universal and transcendent aspects of God involved in all of creation. The Eastern philosophy presented a more positive and constructive approach to God than mainstream Christianity of nineteenth century Western Europe did.

Incidentally, I did not view my creative work as something separate from meditation.

Leichtman: What do you mean?

Wagner: The inspiration which impels genuine creative work automatically attunes you to the divine essence of whatever it is you are doing—the divine essence of music, the divine essence of beauty, and so on. The true creative person is very much aware of being in a more refined state of consciousness than he or she ordinarily enjoys. It is very similar to a meditative state.

Japikse: Yes.

Wagner: Now I know that this would not be a balanced state of meditation such as the two of you would teach; the focus would be exclusively on pursuing creative inspiration, and not on integrating wisdom, love, and higher perspectives into the conscious personality. But it definitely is meditative.

Leichtman: Well, that's fascinating. Is there more you can tell us about what it is like to be caught up in this state of inspiration?

Wagner: Yes, but I can only speak out of my own experience. Other composers and artists might well have very much different experiences.

Very often, when I sat down to compose a piece of music, I would know how the completed piece would sound—even though I had not yet started to write. Or I would know how an entire opera would appear. Mind you, however, this did not make it any easier to write! *[Laughter.]* One can easily be overwhelmed by the volume of ideas, images, sounds, and feelings coming into your awareness all at the same time. It is like a cloudburst of knowable things exploding in your thinking.

Leichtman: What was going through your mind when all this was happening—besides the music?

Wagner: Nothing—I was completely focused in the music. I thought of myself as meditating on it.

Leichtman: Forgive me for pursuing this a bit more, but meditation is a very important topic for me, as you know. What were you meditating on? The essence of the music?

Wagner: Yes, you could say that. And the ultimate source of music.

Leichtman: Which is?

Wagner: God. God's creation, really. I felt in tune with the entire universe when I was working—not so much when I was listening to music being played, but most definitely when I was composing it.

Japikse: Is this sort of experience in any way connected with what some people refer to as the music of the spheres? Is there music of the spheres?

Wagner: Yes, there is. At least a music of sorts. It sounds like thousands of bees playing violins.

Leichtman: Do you mean something like the music which was composed for the movie *2001*?

Wagner: Something on that order, yes. The music of the spheres is actually a background sound—not quite what serves as the inspiration for classical music. Obviously, not all classical music sounds like bees swarming!

The inspiration for classical music generally comes from a specific class of musical themes which "float" about the psychic levels of creation. If you have a capacity for inner hearing, you can tune into a variety of different kinds of musical inspiration. It is not always as easy as this description of it makes it sound, however. Sometimes when we think we are inspired, we are just tuning into the psychic essence of a piece of music which has already been created and played on earth somewhere. This is still an inspiration of sorts—we might even be tuning into the original source—but we are nonetheless not the first to compose that particular theme.

Leichtman: As I recall, the theme you used in the overture to *The Flying Dutchman* was used earlier in a different form by Mendelssohn. It is the exact same melody, except that Mendelssohn made it sound like a soothing lullaby, and you presented it in a heroic style. It is a striking example of how the same theme can be used to create totally different effects.

Wagner: Yes. Of course, some people who don't know very much about the creative process will then accuse us of stealing, which can be very irksome. In this case, I did not think I was doing anything other than creating an original piece. As you say, the effect of the two pieces is totally different in each case. Mendelssohn is a great genius. We respect each other very much.

The inspiration that was available to me—or to many, many other classical composers—is so vast and overwhelming that there is absolutely no need to steal anyone else's ideas. The thought of doing so is repugnant—something that only an untalented amateur would stoop to!

Leichtman: To return for a moment to your personal experiences in the act of composing, it sounds as though these peak moments must have been totally enervating. Did you feel "spaced out," as they say nowadays?

Wagner: I felt as strong as a giant while I was working. I was tremendously focused in what I was doing—not spaced out.

Leichtman: Were you terribly exhausted once you were finished?

Wagner: At the end of it, yes, because I was putting my whole being into the work. I might sit at the piano for hours and write. My body was not doing anything extreme, but I would be drained by the creative exertion.

Leichtman: It almost sounds as though you were

working as a medium might work.

Wagner: I was working exactly as a medium works, except that I was "entertaining" creative inspiration, rather than an individual spook.

Leichtman: How would you describe that creative inspiration? Was it your own spirit? An angel?

Wagner: At the time, I did not know—nor did I care. The artist or musician is always more interested in what he can do with his creative inspiration than in tracking down its source.

Leichtman [chuckling]: That's why we are conducting these interviews—to give people like you the chance to answer questions you were too busy to ask during your physical lifetimes.

Wagner: I see. Well, I suppose it was often a combination of various elements—partly the creative aspect of my own spirit, partly angelic, partly help from people in spirit, and partly the essence of music itself. Creative talent will often attract the assistance and interest of all of these sources, and it's rather difficult to sort it all out and say this theme came from angels and this idea came from spooks.

Leichtman: Suppose a budding composer or musician wanted to invoke inspiration. How should he go about it? What source should he try to contact? An angel? A spirit? His higher self?

Wagner: I don't think that making the contact is nearly as difficult as you are making it out to be. It happens more or less automatically in response to the intent of the individual to do outstanding work. Whenever a genuine call for assistance is sent out into the universe, it is answered. It is always answered. Sometimes a person doesn't like the answer, so he will ignore it and claim his request was overlooked, but all calls are answered—just like prayer. The factor which determines how the call is answered is the level of dedication of the musician or artist or writer—his devotion to beauty and grace, his reverence for elegance and excellence, and his willingness to incorporate these elements into the music, the painting, or the book he is creating.

Leichtman: Ah, so the most powerful invocation is a true dedication to the work you are doing. I guess this means that all those people who struggle to memorize the Hebrew names of angels are just dilettantes.

[Laughter.]

Wagner: Not dilettantes—"would-bes."

Leichtman: Or "has beens."

Wagner: More likely "never weres."

[Guffawing.]

Keep in mind that most of the people you are interviewing in this series were never bothered by the dilettantes in their fields. They just never thought about them.

Leichtman: What more could you tell the young, aspiring composer about developing his creativity?

Wagner: To have talent. *[Laughter.]* I know that sounds a little pompous, but unless you have talent to begin with, even the deepest sincerity in the world will not connect you with the inspiration you need. And talent is something which is acquired by studying and working in a particular field over many lifetimes.

Leichtman: Well, I know that is true, but aren't there certain approaches a creative person will develop to make it easier to contact inspiration? Didn't you go through a ritual of imagining that you were going to entertain God, getting all dressed up and going to your purple room?

Wagner: Oh sure, but that was just a personal trick which helped me attune myself. I wouldn't recommend that for everyone.

Leichtman: Still, I think it is a good example of how you honored the spirit of music.

Wagner: It was my method for tuning into the archetype of music—the essence of music—and then bringing it into my consciousness as a living presence.

I suppose I will have to get technical and use some terms that you might use, but I never used during my physical lifetime. What I was doing by using that little trick was bringing the inspiration "down" to the mental level, so I could quickly write down the basic score and add the emotional lift it needed, before the essence of it escaped my grasp. It was a way of dressing the inspiration up in clothing, if I may put it that way, so I could bring it into manifestation more easily. I don't know how to fully explain it without sounding like Einstein. I invested the inspiration with mental and emotional matter, and because of that, I was able to bring it down from a transcendent to a physical level.

Leichtman: Did you consciously experience specific mental and emotional states while composing—images or moods which reflected the essence of the theme?

Wagner: Of course. You have to feel a mood in order to express it. You have to have a mental idea of the meaning of a scene in order to convey it.

Leichtman: There is a passage in *Siegfried* called "Forest Murmurs" which certainly illustrates that. Just listening to the music conveys a marvelous sense of being in a forest with the sunlight coming through the leaves, the wind making soft rustling sounds, and the birds twittering. The music evokes these impressions and images in my imagination.

Wagner: And that is precisely the kind of rich experience which composers seek to evoke in the audience—even if it is not quite the exact image and effect they experienced themselves while writing.

I believe the Walt Disney movie *Fantasia* did an excellent job of showing how classical music can be transformed into a marvelous show of color and form. And this brings up a topic which deserves more attention. On the inner side of life, where I can now see music as well as hear it, the sounds of classical music are accompanied by all sorts of beautiful, colored forms. A physical person would have to be clairvoyant to see them, but they are just a natural phenomenon at this dimension.

Leichtman: I believe both [C.W.] Leadbeater and Corinne Heline have described the thoughtforms of music in their writings.

Wagner: The label doesn't matter, as long as it is understood that the phenomenon is real. And by ascertaining the quality of these forms and colors, you can roughly judge the quality of the music. As you might expect, the beautiful and harmonious colors and forms are associated with beautiful music—and ugly music produces ugly colors and forms.

Leichtman: Would knowing this be useful to the composer? The reason I ask is that many writers of fiction say they try to visualize very clearly the subjects they are writing about. This helps them breathe life into their stories, because it gives them the sense that they are recording an actual scene. Should the composer try to do the same in terms of visualizing the tone and imagery of the themes he is trying to convey?

Wagner: Absolutely. *[Laughing]* I am not sure that is a brilliant new revelation.

Leichtman: Probably not, but one of the purposes of these interviews is to reveal how inspired geniuses do their work. And I sense the need to dispel the naive notion that inspiration just falls out of the sky like a gold brick.

Wagner: I see your point. No, inspiration does not fall out of the sky, although sometimes it does flow so automatically that you lose all awareness of how it is working—you are so caught up in the life of the inspiration and translating it into your masterpiece of the moment. Keep in mind that I could never have described the creative process as completely as I have just done while I was actually alive and working in a physical body.

Leichtman: Which is precisely why these interviews are so worthwhile, I think.

Let's move on to a different topic. You had some rather ferocious critics during your life. How did criticism affect your work?

Wagner: I suppose anyone who tries to do something innovative—especially on such a grandiose scale as opera—attracts a great amount of commentary.

Leichtman: I do believe most historians would use a stronger word than "commentary." Many considered you a rebel—perhaps a revolutionary—in your day. And that was not always limited just to the field of music, was it? Some of your ideas about the nature of society were revolutionary, too.

Wagner: I was a very intense person. I was also a

bit selfish in some ways, or at least many people considered me selfish. Artistic people tend to be that way.

Leichtman: Why is that?

Wagner: In a way, it is a question of "enlightened selfishness." In order to get his work done, the creative person must protect his time and keep certain people away. When I was doing my work, it consumed me; nothing else was important then.

Japikse: Are there other aspects of this selfishness?

Wagner: Well, the single-mindedness of the creative person is usually misunderstood by people, and artists are often heavily criticized for it. But the intensity required for outstanding creative work demands this kind of single-mindedness. Criticism is the price we pay for it.

I suppose one of the most outstanding features of a creative person is his passion—not necessarily for other people, although I did love several women rather passionately—but for his work. Music wasn't just a job for me—*it was my life!* I talked about the spiritual frenzy of creating a while ago. This kind of passion is a very important part of creativity. But it is very difficult for the average person to comprehend what this passion is like, or how it affects the creative person. So he criticizes without understanding.

Leichtman: Some of your critics actually thought you to be a fanatic, not so much for what you did in music, as for the strong convictions you held on other topics.

Wagner: Well, the passion filtered into all aspects of my life. I couldn't help that. Once any creative person discovers the capacity to touch archetypal levels of inspiration, he is apt to develop strong convictions on all aspects of life. He touches a certain power the average person doesn't deal with.

Leichtman: Which is why creative people sometimes become terribly unbalanced and too narrowly focused.

Wagner: This is one of the risks, certainly. But it is a risk which people should be brave enough to face. There is extra power in the forces of creative inspiration. It can lift you up to great heights, and plunge you down to the lowest depths. If you do not handle it wisely, you can become intensely selfish—or overly reactive to criticism. Many creative people have lost the moorings of their sanity, and had to be hospitalized. Obviously, some handle it better than others. But what is important is learning to follow your own lights and listen to the beat of your own drummer, because the creative person cannot afford to listen to somebody else's drumbeat.

Leichtman: I am grateful for your candor on this topic. I'm a bit uneasy about pressing you too much about your own personal problems—which are, after all, your business and not ours—but I think this is a part of creativity which needs to be better understood. I know many creative people who think the neurotic problems they are struggling with are unique to them. They think they should be both well adjusted and very creative at the same time. I suppose that would be ideal, but from what you have been saying, I gather it is an unlikely combination—at least until humanity as a whole knows more about creativity. My observations of truly gifted and creative people certainly suggest that there can be real problems in working with the very force of inspiration itself.

Well, I'd like to leave all of this probing of the creative psyche behind and get back to the subject of music itself. Let me ask you a question which may be impossible to answer, since it covers such a vast territory. What is the real significance of music? Why is it important to humanity?

Wagner: Music is one of the great civilizing forces of humanity. It lifts us away from the animal state—far, far away—all the way to the sublime level of spirit. Music heals. It heals the personality and even the soul. Music soothes. It inspires. It fills us with beauty and joy. In other words, *it makes us more than human,* if I dare to be so bold as to put it that way. Music—good music—must be considered as one of the ways God speaks to earth!

Now, to be fair—and I'm getting some prodding from my friends up here—all of the arts collectively are designed to serve as a means of inspiring humanity. Good paintings, sculpture, and literature all play a role in refining and civilizing humanity, along with good music. All of the arts serve to spiritualize humanity in very important ways.

The *unique* role that music plays is more difficult to describe. Music communicates its message directly to the subconscious. It can stir up an effect in the listener even if he doesn't consciously understand what he is experiencing.

You have to think about a book to be moved by it. You have to follow the plot of a play to make sense of it. Even in responding to art, you need to reflect on the content of a painting to get its message. But with music, it is possible to be profoundly affected without giving it much conscious thought. It comes to you immediately, directly. None of the other arts quite achieve this effect.

I do not mean to imply, however, that it doesn't help to think about good music—or that good musicians can be stupid. That is not true at all! The role of the mind is very important in understanding and appreciating good music. Yet there is also a soundless essence to music which conveys much of the beauty and enriching influence of music. It can communicate directly with the subconscious, bypassing—if necessary—the listener's lack of conscious attention or understanding.

Leichtman: What is this soundless essence? I think I know what you mean, as I have experienced it, but how would you explain it?

Wagner: It's the inner life or inner force of music, the "pure music" that has spoken to the composer, speaks through the musician, and now communicates directly to the subconscious of the listener. To use esoteric terminology, it would be the mental and emotional elements of the music. I refer to it as "soundless" because it is not part of the music actually produced by the physical instruments. It is not ordinarily heard, unless the listener is quite clairaudient. But just because it is not heard by almost everyone doesn't mean that it isn't there. It is, and it touches people who hear the music on subconscious levels.

Leichtman: You are talking about a psychic essence, then. At least, that would be my term for it.

Wagner: Yes.

Leichtman: Okay. You mentioned that part of the purpose of music is to refine and enrich civilization. What are the ennobling effects of good music? How does good music have this spiritualizing effect?

Wagner: It strikes chords in the structure of the subconscious mind, and can actually change the patterns of your thought, feeling, and association. This, in turn, can lead to many other changes. And so, good music can literally be healing, uplifting, and spiritualizing—just as the wrong kind of music can be destructive.

Japikse: Are these chords objective or subjective? I would presume that to some degree they would be objective, since the psychic essence would be the same for everyone hearing a piece, even though each person might well react individually, subjectively.

Wagner: The psychic essence of the music is objective, yes. And the capacity of any piece of music to refine consciousness would be roughly the same for everyone listening to it, regardless of his or her personal reactions to it.

Leichtman: That's fascinating. Some experts claim that composers can be classified by the kind of subtle effect they have on the listener. Beethoven, for example, is said to generate a mood or psychological climate of sympathy which saturates the whole being of the listener. And this happens whether or not you are listening directly to it, or the music just happens to be in the background.

Wagner: Well, that is true, although I'm not sure I would describe Beethoven's music in quite that way. I would say that the dominant chord Beethoven's music strikes is the indwelling nobility of our humanity. But mind you, it is dangerous to generalize, because that should be the effect of all good classical music. And it is hardly possible to sum up the creative genius of Beethoven in a single theme. There are many chords in consciousness that Beethoven's music strikes.

Leichtman: Oh, absolutely. Beethoven's sixth symphony is remarkably different from the almost belligerent fifth or the joyous ninth. The inner essence of any masterpiece will obviously have its own unique characteristics. And yet there is a common theme to his music.

Wagner: Yes. A common effect or impact. I guess it would be the real genius of the composer.

Leichtman: Well, if you don't mind, I would like to ask you about the dominant themes of other major composers, both to check out my own impressions and to help illustrate the basic point we've been talking about. I know this would only be a general observation on the impact of the music of these composers, but I think it would be interesting.

Wagner: Okay.

Leichtman: It is said that listening to Chopin promotes a sense of refinement and a capacity to discern and appreciate subtle shades and degrees of anything delicate.

Wagner: I think that would be obvious to most people listening to his music.

Leichtman: And that Brahms promotes a charitable and nurturing attitude toward life.

Wagner: I would call it more a note of human kindness, sometimes cheerfulness.

Leichtman: What about Mendelssohn?

Wagner: The best simple answer would be joy. There is a strong devotional quality to his music. Most of it, you know, has a religious theme somewhere in the background. He was a very spiritual man—a mystic first and then a composer, in the real sense of those terms. If anyone was ever conscious of angels aiding him with his inspiration, it had to be Mendelssohn.

Leichtman: What about Sibelius? I can't quite figure him out. He seems to be strongly connected to the forces of nature.

Wagner: The stature and nobility of nature, but in its brooding silence and perseverance, its awesome grandeur and simplicity. He also reflected something of the ruggedness and hardiness of his country and its people [Finland].

Debussy and Stravinsky use themes related to the forces of nature, too, but they are entirely different themes. Stravinsky taps the raw vigor and vitality of nature rising up out of the earth; Debussy, in some of his pieces, captures a lyrical aspect of gamboling, playful nature spirits. I'm thinking of *La Mer* in particular. Ravel did something similar in *Daphnis and Chloe,* although that piece has other aspects as well which clearly depict a rapturous state of people taking delight in each other's company and life itself—more delight in life per se than anything else.

Leichtman: What about some of the modern Russian composers, such as Prokofiev, Shostakovich, and Khachaturian? When I listen to their works, I feel as though I am groaning with courage, perseverance, and steadfastness.

Wagner: Judging from your persistence in pursuing this particular line of questioning, I would say you may have even *overdosed* on Prokofiev, Shostakovich, and Khachaturian! *[Laughter.]*

Many composers draw a certain inspiration from the culture they live in. The national spirit is one of the many strong conditioning influences in the type of music that is created. And I would agree with you that courage, perseverance, and steadfastness—even to the point of groaning—is part of the chord of the Russian spirit.

Japikse: It even comes through much of Russian literature.

Wagner: Yes. And one of the most interesting ways to discern the impact of a national spirit on music is to study the works of composers who travel abroad and then produce very distinctive compositions based on their visits to other countries. I am thinking of Dvorak, for instance—Mendelssohn, too.

Leichtman: Hmmm. Let me throw you two more names and then we'll get on to other subjects. How about Mozart and Bach?

Wagner: Mozart is often playful, and he consistently promotes an elegance of the mind. In that sense, he is somewhat like Chopin, but while Chopin's music encourages refinement and gracefulness, Mozart strikes a slightly different chord—almost formal elegance. I might even say there is a touch of flamboyance in Mozart. But again, this is an oversimplification. Being able to deal first-hand with the essence of music as I am now, I am used to working with the whole fabric and magnificence of these musical works, and it is hard to condense such range and scope into a few select qualities. I find myself wanting to add more and more qualifications.

Leichtman: I understand.

Wagner: It's part of the richness of their music. Now Bach impresses me as having touched the essence of religion. A tone of worship and reverence runs through most of his work. Of course, much of the music he wrote was commissioned by the church.

Leichtman: Hmmm, the essence of religion. I suppose you're right in terms of the music he wrote for the church, but what about his secular compositions? I am thinking of the preludes and fugues in *The Well-Tempered Clavier*. These pieces seem to have a tremendously stimulating effect on the mind, enriching the capacity for logic, order, and mental precision.

Wagner: Well, they had that effect on the development of music, too. Bach is a good example of the difficulty inherent in categorizing the life work of a composer in a word or two. It really cannot be done—although it is fun to try.

Leichtman: I appreciate the limitation, but I'm glad we tried. I think it's important to give actual examples of the dramatic and psychological impact good music can have, and to show that music is something more than mere entertainment. It has an inherent value.

Let me shift subjects now. Suppose you were to give a lecture to students of music appreciation. What would you say to them? Is there a skill to listening to music?

Wagner: I would tell them that music—good music—has a much deeper and longer impact than is suspected. Music has a capacity to remain in the mind long after it has ceased to exist in the ear, and that enhances the power of music. It also means that we must take this into account in listening to and appreciating music. Sometimes the music remains in the mind in the form of fond memories that are replayed as a mental sound; at other times, it is just a general memory of the quality or impact of the music.

Leichtman: Perhaps I should interrupt for a moment and ask you to define "good music."

Wagner: There are many ways of doing that, but the

simplest test of good music is its capacity to uplift your spirits. Good music stimulates the nobility in your character, while bad music does the opposite. You would probably say that good music helps the individual to integrate with his spiritual qualities.

Leichtman: All right.

Wagner: But let's return to the question of the skills of appreciating music. There are several different levels at which we listen to music—the mental, emotional, and physical levels. But listening at the physical level is fairly automatic, so there are actually two major levels at which music can be appreciated, the intellectual and the emotional. A person who wants to get the full benefit from listening to music should be able to appreciate it at both levels. He should have a fair intellectual grasp of the mechanics of the piece—that is, how it is put together, the theories and rules by which the piece was created, and the basic idea the music entails. But at the same time, he needs to learn to interact emotionally with the music—to respond to the music on the astral level.

"Astral" is not a word I commonly used.

[Laughter.]

Leichtman: What did you call it?

Wagner: The beauty and joy of the music—the substance of the music, as opposed to the mechanics of it.

Leichtman: I think you had the better term.

Wagner: I'm getting the technical esoteric jargon fed to me by a thesaurus in human form over here.

Japikse: The spirit of Roget, no doubt. *[Laughter.]*

Wagner: Not exactly. Now, the astral or emotional perception of the beauty and qualities associated with a piece tends to be highly individualistic, because it is a subjective response based on one's personal perspective. But as we have just been discussing, there is also an inherent emotional tone which is independent of the conscious reaction of the listener.

Leichtman: And so just as a C sharp is a C sharp even if you happen to be deaf, Beethoven's *Ode to Joy* is still joyful even if you happen to be depressed.

Wagner: Right. Now, the key to appreciating good music in its fullest is to integrate the mental and emotional responses, placing them in harmony and perceiving them together. The person who appreciates music primarily on an intellectual level or primarily on an emotional level is definitely missing something. Music speaks to both the intellect and the emotions.

Of course, there is yet another level of appreciating music that the enlightened individual can respond to, and that is the spiritual essence of the music. By using the contact he has developed with his own soul, the enlightened person can tune into the divine essence—what you call the archetypal force—of the music. This is a higher octave than the psychic essence we were talking about earlier.

I would venture to say that this would be the ultimate in music appreciation.

Leichtman: Yes. It is certainly easy to do that with the works of Beethoven, Gustav Mahler, the heroic themes of Bruckner, and of course your music. These works have a tremendous impact.

Wagner: There is a crew of angels whose specific task is to maintain the quality of music on all levels—the level of the soul, the mental level, and the emotional or astral level. Maintaining the quality and impact of music is part of their training—and part of their work. They are like the gardeners and supporters of music. So the highest form of musical appreciation would be to nurture and support the quality of music somewhat in the same way. But there are many levels of musical appreciation leading up to that.

If you are able to appreciate music at this level, it can become a powerful influence in your life, not limited just to the composition you hear. You begin to associate it with everything you do and think and feel, either consciously or subconsciously. This is why I started my comments on the appreciation of music with the observation that its impact is deeper and endures longer than is commonly suspected.

Of course, this kind of perception can enhance the actual act of listening to music, too. The more evolved a person is, especially if he is blessed with clairvoyance, the more he can tune into the beauty of the music. Normally the perception of the beauty of music is non-visual, but as we suggested earlier, a clairvoyant can actually see it—and it is an astounding sight, especially if angels are at work.

Leichtman: You are suggesting now that the angels help not only in the composition of a piece, but also at times in the performance of it?

Wagner: Yes. In great classical music, it is not uncommon for angels to assist in the work of organizing the production and inspiring the conductor and the musicians. When this is happening, the orchestra seems to blend together in a symphony of beautiful colored lights as well as sound. As the music proceeds, these streams of light, which are the counterpart of the musical themes and phrases, build up into a progressively larger and more complex form. This form keeps changing, sometimes resembling beautiful architecture, sometimes appearing like elaborately carved ivory with jewels and precious metals. At other times, it may resemble blooming flowers intermixed with colored crystals. And all of it is moving and evolving, some parts flashing by very quickly, and other aspects enduring for quite some time. In some ways, it resembles what you see in the better quality kaleidoscopes as you keep the tiny colored particles moving. The whole effect can be quite fascinating and beautiful on several levels.

Leichtman: It sounds like it. Would it help if the listener tried to listen to the music in a light meditative state, so he or she could tune into some of these deeper levels as well as the physical sounds?

Wagner: Actually, I suppose the composer and the musicians have not really done their work unless the *music* puts the listener into an altered state of consciousness. But yes, I would encourage the person who wants to fully appreciate a piece of music to listen in a light meditative state—to throw himself into the essence of the music, so to speak.

Leichtman: Should the listener make an effort to seek out the archetypal theme of the music—the essence that gives rise both to the emotional and mental aspects of the music? In your operas, for instance, it is very clear to me that you are inspired by the archetypal themes of heroism and aspiration and the struggle to overcome tremendous hardships to achieve redemption. Being able to interact with these forces while I am listening to your music greatly enriches its power and meaning to me. Would this be one way a lover of music could orient his or her search for beauty and meaning while listening to music?

Wagner: Yes, I would recommend that. I think the value of this idea is especially clear in opera, where you have both a story and music. This is why opera is difficult to carry out successfully—you have to integrate both the music and the story effectively, in a manner and style that will honor the underlying themes of the opera. But some opera fans all but dismiss the story as irrelevant, claiming that the music alone is the real substance. In most cases, these are people who are looking to music as entertainment alone; they are not interested in the themes and the message the music presents. They just don't bother to try to grasp the story and the plot, or what they signify. I find it difficult to appreciate the full range of opera on that basis.

The same principle applies to all music, of course, not just to opera. There is an inner archetypal theme which is the source of beauty and meaning for the piece. Listening to music in a light meditative state and trying to tune into this archetypal quality is an excellent way to deepen the richness of your appreciation of music.

Leichtman: I remember seeing a film of Isaac Stern teaching a group of violin students. They were very nervous about performing for him, and he was trying to relax them. So he said they should first feel the joy and sense the music in here, pointing to his head, and if they could do that, he said, then they would also be able to express this joy in the way they played. It seemed to me that the good listener should try to do the same.

Wagner: Oh my, yes. He should try to internalize the experience of the music as much as possible. Unless you can appreciate music in your mind first, you cannot really appreciate what you hear with your ears.

Leichtman: Since you mentioned that angels do assist in the performance of certain great classical pieces, let me ask you this. Why are some performances so dull, even though they are technically correct? What factors make the difference? Are the musicians not in tune with the spirit of the music? Are the angels taking the night off? *[Laughter.]* Is the conductor not in contact with his higher self?

Wagner: There could be a variety of reasons for a dull performance. Sometimes the musicians are just having a bad night.

As a general rule, the more the orchestra is tuned into the spirit of the music being played, the better the performance will be. This does not have much to do with the overall spiritual development of the musicians; it is more a factor of professionalism. I don't mean to imply that the spiritual evolution does not figure into how well an individual might be able to perform; it does. But some musicians have an ability to bypass all of the interferences of their character flaws when they perform music, and tune in directly to the spirit of the music. They may know nothing about the life of spirit and meditating, but when they are performing, they get in touch with the essence of music. The ability to do that performance after performance—and not to be dull—would be the hallmark of the true professional.

Leichtman: I'm afraid I interrupted your comments on appreciating music. There's probably more we ought to ask about that. Do you think it would be helpful to listen to a recording of a symphony before going to a concert at which it will be performed, or refreshing your memory of the plot of an opera before going to see it?

Wagner: Listening to a recording of the music that is going to be performed in a concert is probably not a good idea. Too many people would end up wasting their time comparing one performance to the other, and that would take away from the enjoyment of the live performance. Reading a short synopsis of the plot of an opera, on the other hand, can help familiarize you with the basic themes, especially if the opera is being performed in a language you don't understand.

I would rather address the need for educating yourself about music in general than in prescribing ways to prepare yourself for a specific concert or opera. This means developing skills in responding to the intellectual content and structure of music, and not just enjoying it emotionally. Except for professional students of music, most people who go to concerts or the opera go for the emotional enjoyment. They do not pay much attention to the mechanical side of music. These people should spend some time learning more about the intellectual beauty and richness which is woven into the great works of music, so they can be moved mentally as well as emotionally. There are many good books available which describe this, or they could take a short course at their local college. The more you grasp the structure of music, the more its richness and refinement can be appreciated.

Leichtman: Can this be overdone? I was listening recently to a series of lectures by Leonard Bernstein on the syntax of music. He was looking at music as a language with rules and traditions of its own. But to get his point across, he had to begin by teaching on general semantics. And then step by step he compared music to poetry, with its rhyming and repetition. It was a brilliant discussion, but I thought it took some of the joy and beauty out of the music. It sounded as though he was treating music as an engineering problem.

Wagner: Well, the intellectual side of music can be overdone, yes. That is true in all art forms. I am told you don't care much for paintings which consist of a rectangular blob of gray with vertical black stripes running down the middle.

Leichtman: No, I think they are pedestrian, if they are art at all.

Wagner: Exactly. This kind of "art" leans so heavily on the mechanics of producing a design that it misses the basic point of art, which is to be beautiful. And the same thing can happen in music, too. But that is not a reason for ignoring the structure and intellectual content of music.

Leichtman: No, but I do think some of the modern composers have gone overboard in stressing the technical side of composition. I'm thinking of some of the pieces of [Arnold] Schoenberg and [Charles] Ives and a host of unknowns.

Wagner: There definitely are those who go too far in adhering to self-made rules and rigid formulas, instead of listening to their inspiration, and this drives the beauty out of music. But others create beautiful sounds which go nowhere—they do not develop the beautiful melodies into any structure or pattern of richness, or interweaving themes, or anything. Both extremes fall short of the ideal. The great composer, obviously, would strive to weave a balance between the technical and the feeling side of music.

Leichtman: Let me ask you about some modern musical creations which seem to have no beauty at all, no discernible melody. In fact, they sound like hammers clanging in a boiler factory at midnight or two dozen machines all beeping at me at once. This is considered avant-garde classical music, but I wonder if it can even be called music? It is mostly stuff written in the past twenty years or so by college professors.

Wagner: The best way to discuss the value of these works as music is to look at the level of your emotional focus as you listen to them. Most people live in a rather narrow range of emotions, expressing themselves within that range and responding primarily to phenomena which are in harmony with that level. Since the purpose of music is to refine consciousness and spiritualize thought and feeling, the best music would be that which lifts you up to a higher emotional focus. Music that drags you down to a lower range would be less desirable. The avant-garde music you are talking about is probably inspired by a lower emotional focus than you are accustomed to. You might liken it to African music and native rumblings or something like that.

Leichtman: I think native rumblings would actually be better. At least they would have a natural rhythm.

Wagner: Yes. Well, the music you are complaining about is an extreme case. It has been approached purely on an intellectual basis with the idea of creating new sounds, new rhythms, and new intellectual sensations, without any regard for emotional content, beauty, and grace.

Leichtman: But if it gives you a headache, what good is it?

Wagner: Obviously not much. The inspiration is

muted or even deadened. The type of person who would create or enjoy listening to this kind of music would probably be very pedantic intellectually and have stunted emotions.

Leichtman: Well, phooey on them. *[Laughter.]* There is so much music which is mentally stimulating and beautiful, too—the music of Bach or Mozart or Haydn, to name just a few—that I don't see why we should waste our time trying to imitate the sound of a boiler factory at midnight. Does that sound so strange?

Wagner: No, not at all. I agree with you.

Leichtman: Well, that's a relief. *[Laughter.]* I thought you might try to talk me into liking it.

Wagner: Bad music is bad music. I wouldn't even think of defending it.

Leichtman: Well, now that you've mentioned bad music, perhaps this would be a good place to chat about the harmful effects of bad music. What can you say about the potentially harmful side of music?

Wagner: Let me begin with a very general statement. Every individual has a duty to filter the information that goes into his subconscious, just as he might filter or screen out the material he eats or drinks. We know full well that certain foods are bad for us and that certain substances are poisonous, and so we exercise reasonable caution about what we put in our mouths. In the same way, I think we should be just as careful to screen the music we allow to enter the subconscious. As I have stated, music has the capacity to enter the subconscious directly, and this fact puts an extra responsibility on us to be cautious regarding what we listen to. I might say something similar about literature, good and bad, but I will confine myself to music.

You know, it is said that the most intimate act that people do together is not X-rated—it is the simple act of having a conversation, because it alters the mind. Music also alters the mind, perhaps even more powerfully and permanently than conversing. That may sound dire to some people, but I mean it as a warning. Not all composers and musicians respect the intimacy of music or the impact it can have. But good composers are careful in what they write, because they do respect the minds of the people who will listen to their music. They use music to uplift, not to poison.

Leichtman: Should we be concerned about the background music we hear in stores while shopping—or even the music from our neighbor's radio or stereo? There's a lot of music we hear but don't really pay attention to. Does that still have an effect on us, even though we are ignoring it?

Wagner: You may consciously ignore music, but if you are physically within range of it, music will not ignore your subconscious. Quite often, the effect of the music is subliminal. The music that is piped through a department store, after all, is designed to have a calming effect on the customer, so he or she will shop more leisurely and linger long enough to purchase additional items. Music can also be used in this way to promote ideas and sway your opinion. As it enters the subconscious, it often brings many ideas and associations with it. It is one of the easier ways to brainwash the public.

Leichtman: Can music alone accomplish this, or does planting a specific message require lyrics?

Wagner: It can happen either way, although music without lyrics would convey more of an intended emotional response than specific ideas. In other words, we still have the two basic levels of music—the emotional response to it, and the idea or theme it conveys. In classical music, the emotional response is meant to be to the archetypal theme of the music, and the primary idea of the composer is usually wrapped up in creating a technical structure which does this. But as you get away from the highly complex structures of classical music, the situation changes somewhat. In a tone poem, for example, the idea can be clearly found in the music. In popular music, the music itself contains mostly a stimulus for an emotional response, not a clear message or idea. It would be necessary to have lyrics.

Leichtman: Well, some types of rock music convey a theme of rebelliousness, hedonism, and self-centeredness. At least this is the message I get from them, and I don't think this is just my reaction. It seems to be inherent in the music.

Wagner: It really isn't inherent in the music so much as it is in the lyrics. The music itself tends to churn up the subconscious in the same way violent and emotionally disruptive surroundings do. That should be obvious.

Leichtman: Wouldn't that be a nonverbal message, though? Maybe I shouldn't try to call it an "idea," but something powerful is being transmitted through the music.

Wagner: Yes, and quite often it is most unpleasant. Now, we must distinguish some rock music from others. There are *some* fine musicians who use the rock and roll medium well, and they are good artists. I don't want to condemn the whole of rock music. However, I would say that the majority of rock and roll music is disruptive and has a negative influence on people. It is violent music which churns the emotions of those listening to it to the point where they begin to have a physical response and behave in violent ways. Sometimes these people even lose control of their physical nature because the response to the music is so strong.

This alone is bad enough, but when you also realize that the lyrics which accompany this violent emotional music often are designed to put the seeds of rebellious or hedonistic ideas into the subconscious, you can quickly see how very negative the whole experience is. I am describing this as I see it now from my perspective on the inner side of life.

Leichtman: I know the thoughtforms created by this kind of music are certainly very ugly, and are bound to have ugly effects on people.

Wagner: I can assure you that no angels participate in the creation or the performance of rock and roll music. *[Laughter.]*

Leichtman: What about these recent discoveries that certain records and tapes contain hidden messages in the lyrics? Apparently phrases were played backwards in the recording so that they are heard in the reverse by the listener. Some of these statements are reported to be very negative—some even promoting devil worship. Can such reversed statements have a subliminal effect on the subconscious?

Wagner: As I have said, music provides an open door to the subconscious. So any message which is being carried by the music also goes directly to the subconscious, where it will be either beneficial or destructive, depending on the quality of the music and the intent of the message. I would assume that very devious types of people are able to use this type of trick to control others—and in fact, *it is being done!*

Keep in mind, however, that it would be extremely difficult to convey a negative message through beautiful music. I don't want readers to become afraid to listen to good music, for fear that the music will open the subconscious and then some other message will shoot through it without them knowing it. You can't have a disruptive or negative message hidden in lofty musical themes. But conversely, if the music tends to be disruptive or chaotic, it is probably safe to assume that the message is too, even when the lyrics do not seem to indicate that. The disruptive music and the negative message go together.

And it is not difficult to test the quality of the music you are listening to. Just test your response to it. If the music lifts you up, it is probably wholesome. If you have a negative response to it, it is probably harmful.

Leichtman: But obviously many people seem to like and respond favorably to music that I would clearly define as disruptive—the kind of music that churns up the subconscious.

Wagner: Yes, there are some people who do get excited and like the strong sensation of violent music, but they are actually responding to the subliminal threat of violence inherent in the music, and that is not a healthy type of excitement. It doesn't really lift them up to a higher level—it just stirs up their baser passions.

Leichtman: Along that line, an interesting experiment on the effect of music was recently made at a maternity hospital in England. They played music to the newborn babies and found that classical pieces such as Brahms' *Lullaby* had a soothing and calming effect, but when they played rock and roll, the babies cried and fussed. Of course, these were infants who had no verbal ability or the intellectual ability to interpret the music— or even an established pattern of psychological conditioning to train them in a specific response. They were simply responding to the innate quality of the music itself.

Wagner: Sure. That makes sense to me.

Leichtman: And then there are the experiments which have been done to demonstrate the effect of music on plants. Rock and roll music killed the plants while classical music made them thrive.

Wagner: And people need to consider whether or not they want that kind of influence running around loose in their subconscious.

One of the things about rock and roll that I find interesting, as I look at music from this side, is that occasionally one of the hard rockers will have a stroke of brilliance and be inspired enough to write what amounts to a beautiful song, with lovely music and inspiring lyrics. And the subconscious responds to these occasional jewels in a very much different way than it reacts to the usual violent rock. It is odd that a group which promotes drugs and hedonism and revolution will suddenly produce a marvelous song about the beauties of nature or some other lofty theme, but it does happen. It really isn't rock and roll at all, even though it is composed and performed by a rock group. It becomes a more acceptable piece of music.

And then the next song on the album, of course, goes right back to smashing the emotions. *[Laughter.]*

What I am saying is that rock and roll per se is not bad. It is the perversion of the medium which is bad. Rock music does have the potential to be very uplifting, even if that potential is seldom realized. It is not the mode of music that creates the problem; it is the consciousness of the individuals who tend to use the medium. We ought to make that clear. In fact, I think I could write a very fine rock and roll song. *[Laughter.]*

Leichtman: I would want to be there to see the pen exploding in your hand as you tried it. *[More laughter.]* But I get your point—the medium itself is not rotten, just the way it's used.

Wagner: And having said that, I want to repeat my warning that you must be very careful what you permit to enter your subconscious. When you listen to music, it is important to consciously make a decision as to whether it is healthy for you or not. If you fail to do this, you may find that you have let a big bunch of junk into your subconscious, and you will have to spend a lot of time clearing it out again. There are ways to clean it out, of course, but it is better not to let the junk come in at all.

Of course, the greatest danger is when people open themselves up even more with drugs. Taking drugs is the equivalent of opening up the subconscious without reserving the ability to close it again—there is no conscious control. A nondrugged person has a great advantage over the individual on drugs, in that he can consciously deal with negative messages which might come from violent forms of music. He has considerable self-control over his mental state. But a drugged person does not have this control. So listening to rock and roll music in a drugged state is something like opening up your subconscious mind and handing it over to the musicians—it is an invitation to serious subconscious manipulation. In fact, it is hard for me to imagine a worse situation. The natural self-defenses that are available to you for mental protection have been suspended by taking the drugs; you have no conscious ability to filter the subliminal impressions which come in with the music.

Now you, Doctor, could listen to some violent rock and roll music with a repulsive message and consciously say to yourself, "This is a bunch of garbage." And you would turn it off. It would have no permanent impact in your subconscious, even though it might damage your emotional aura, if you were forced to listen to it for very long. But you could take care of that later on. However, when someone who will not reject this garbage—either because he likes it or, even worse, because he's on drugs and *can't* reject it—listens to such music, it is a very dangerous situation. There is the real threat of long-term manipulation of his thinking and emotions.

Leichtman: What are the long-range effects?

Wagner: Low self-esteem, irresponsible behavior, selfishness, and the erosion of consciousness. Over a period of time, it can be almost as damaging to the personality as drugs. You can frequently see this in the performers themselves—there is often a lot of brutality and bad taste on stage. This is just another sign of the harmful effects of this kind of music. Performers of classical music certainly don't suffer a deterioration in consciousness and good taste from the music they play.

You would think more people would make note of this fact.

Japikse: Along this same line, what about other forms of popular music in America? One that was popular not long ago was disco music, and there is—

Leichtman: Country and western?

Japikse: I was thinking of jazz.

Wagner: I can appreciate some aspects of country and western because it deals with real people and real problems. But the music itself is unimaginative.

Leichtman: So much of country and western is just whining and complaining, though. It's depressing because it puts so much emphasis on problems.

Wagner: Yes, the overall effect is not very uplifting, but some of it is quite good. Disco music, on the other hand, is rather artificial. It has no message or anything—just a rapid beat and crisp sound. It basically helps you short-circuit your brain so you can be foolish for a couple of hours. *[Laughter.]*

Leichtman: What about the effect of the environment in which disco music is usually played? I refer to the flashing lights and very loud volume of the music.

Wagner: Disco dancing is only a modern revival of primitive tribal dances designed to generate animal lust through the hypnotic rhythm of the drums—with flashing lights thrown in to enhance the hypnotic effect. Does this answer your question?

Leichtman: I think of disco music *only* as a cure for a deficiency in schizophrenia and mania. *[Laughter.]*

Japikse: What about jazz?

Wagner: I would consider jazz a type of popular music, perhaps a refinement of it in some ways. Before jazz, most popular music was rather maudlin and sentimental.

Japikse: Does jazz have any of the beneficial effects that classical music does?

Wagner: Some forms of it can, yes. Jazz was designed primarily to stimulate its listeners in certain ways, primarily to add to a party atmosphere in speakeasies. Drinking and jazz commonly went together in those days, and I think they still do in modern times. At least jazz is more intelligently thought through than disco music or rock and roll.

Japikse: Damned with faint praise! *[Laughter.]*

Wagner: Yes.

Leichtman: How about the lyrics of popular music other than disco and rock and roll?

Wagner: The voice in much popular music is often something of an independent instrument, and some of the songs which become quite popular create a very pleasant effect. I doubt if anyone pays much attention to the lyrics of disco or rock and roll. They are there primarily to add to the cacophony. Despite this, however, the subconscious *will* hear those lyrics and take in the message, which is precisely why there is more danger in that type of music.

Leichtman: Suppose someone wanted to use music to enrich his consciousness. What kind of music should he use and how should he go about it? Let's take first the person who has overdosed on bad music and wants to repair the damage, and second, the person who is already someone with good values and spiritual intentions who wants to use music to enhance his reverence for life, patience, courage, compassion, and so on.

Wagner: In the case of the person who has overdosed on bad music, it would depend on the effect it has had on his subconscious.

Leichtman: Well, let's suppose this person has a chronic problem with depression. What music would you suggest he play to cheer him up?

Wagner: Something light and bouncy. I would not

recommend that he listen to anything complex or intellectually heavy in the sense of the loud, boisterous stuff I have been known to write—nothing Wagnerian for this person, at least in the beginning. He needs something light, airy, melodic, and calm. Perhaps something written by Ravel or Debussy.

Leichtman: But not Mahler's eighth symphony?

Wagner: Oh no! This person needs light, airy music for awhile, not to be zapped by the voices of hundreds of singers and a huge orchestra blasting you with joy. Now this isn't to say that you wouldn't eventually progress to something like that, but you would prescribe a series of pieces which would begin with the simple and progress to the complex and rich.

Leichtman: Would it be useful for this person to meditate on some kind of image or symbol which would enhance the attempt to feel cheerful and optimistic?

Wagner: Sure. He could think of a joyful memory or joyful person, or just try to see and feel himself being joyful. You wouldn't expect the music to do all the work while he just sat there and soaked it up passively.

Leichtman: This does suggest that there are endless applications for the use of music in this way.

Wagner: Sure. Eventually there will be musicians who will write specific music for specific ailments, and a music doctor who will prescribe the right doses for you.

Leichtman: I see. Music for a sprained wrist, music for gallstones. *[Laughter.]* Are you serious?

Wagner: Sure.

Leichtman: Well, it does make sense. I remember reading about Albert Schweitzer before I interviewed him *[Schweitzer Returns]*, and how at one point in his life he was experiencing a writing block. So he went off to listen to one of your operas—*Tannhauser,* I believe—and was so inspired and energized by it that he wrote all through the night and into the next morning in a frenzy of creative output. The music must have been a wonderful stimulus for him.

Am I correct in assuming that music affects mainly our consciousness as opposed to the body?

Wagner: For the most part, music has its main effect on the state of the mind and the emotions. Music is a type of vibration, and as such, it can readily affect the subtle matter and vibrations of our mental and emotional bodies. But as the mental and emotional bodies experience change, the health of the physical body can be affected, too.

Leichtman: There are people who make the claim that chanting and mumbling in certain ways can have a direct effect on the body.

Wagner: To a certain extent, they do. But repetitive sounds are something most people soon stop listening to.

Leichtman: I don't want to sound absurd, but some of these people claim that they have a certain chant for prostate trouble, another chant for the liver, and so on.

Wagner: Well, it keeps them out of mischief, I guess.

Leichtman: Will we ever have something like they had in the early days of ancient Egypt, where sound and color were used as major ways of healing people?

Wagner: Yes, we will. And the Egyptians also used sound to move giant pieces of stone. I can't quite explain how it was done, but sound was involved.

Leichtman: They chanted instead of using musical instruments, didn't they?

Wagner: Yes, they chanted, but they also used a device which resembled a tuning fork. It was struck and then held to propel a piece of stone.

Leichtman: We could use a handy gadget like that now. It would help with the energy crisis.

Wagner: Someone is telling me that it is possible to adapt one of Nikola Tesla's ideas and develop a motor that will operate on sound instead of fuel.

Leichtman: Don't you mean electricity and an electric motor?

Wagner: No, it will be more related to sound.

Japikse: Cars will run on ordinary mantras?

[Laughter.]

Leichtman: Or maybe on Wagnerian overtures. Of course, if that were the case, the car might turn purple and go off in search of the holy grail, instead of heading for the local department store. *[More laughter.]*

Japikse: And *The Flying Dutchman* could put you out at sea for decades, when all you wanted to do was drive to the post office.

Leichtman: They would have to put warnings on cars, "This vehicle runs only on non-Wagnerian music."

[Guffawing.]

Wagner: Well, I think we've run our comments on the healing qualities of music into the ground. As for the second part of your question, the use of music to strengthen values and spiritual intentions, you might want to explore some of the classical music of the East, as well as the great music of the West. Because the East has had a stronger spiritual tradition than the West for some time, they have done more to combine the spiritual life with their music, and a good deal of the music of the East has become a spiritual expression, almost a meditation in musical form. Not all of it's accessible to the Western person, because it would be necessary to move aside the cultural differences of the East and the West to fully appreciate it. But if those differences can be overcome, there is a great deal of music, especially in India, that is designed to enrich and stimulate spiritual awareness and the qualities of the spiritual life.

In the West, we've had to be more circumspect about introducing spiritual themes into music. There was a time when much of our classical music was commissioned by the church, and some of that certainly has a strong effect on the spiritual nature. But in many cases, the music which has the strongest potential for awakening spiritual qualities can be found in music composed for the opera and the concert hall. I worked very hard to inject spiritual elements into my music, and I know many other composers have, too. Well, we talked about a number of them earlier.

I am told that there are a number of composers in America today who are working toward the same ideal. Some of their work is quite good, some is mediocre, but they are musicians who are trying to live a spiritual life and use their music as a spiritual tool, not just as an outlet for themselves but to stimulate spiritual qualities in others.

Leichtman: I have a question about an instrument used in much of the music from India. It creates a continuous sound that goes "owoww-owoww-owoww." Is that kind of sound conducive to music with a spiritual theme? I find it rather unpleasant.

Wagner: It can be, yes. It depends on the individual who is playing it, the piece he is playing, and your own cultural attunement. You are probably responding to the strangeness of the sound, which is not a familiar one to your Western ears.

Leichtman: I much prefer lovely Japanese kyoto music, which is also played on a stringed instrument and is from a different culture.

Wagner: Keep in mind that individual taste makes a great difference in the final response.

Leichtman: I have the impression that different instruments affect consciousness in different ways. For instance, if you take a violin concerto and transcribe it for the flute, which is often done, it comes out not just sounding differently, but also affecting the mind and the emotions differently.

Wagner: Absolutely.

Leichtman: The flute seems to stimulate the mental as well as the emotional levels, while the violin affects me primarily at the heart level. I suppose flute music has a greater potential to be healing and enriching to the mind than violin music does.

Wagner: And this is why the good composer does not tie himself down to a single instrument, but chooses from a wide array of instruments to create the varying effect he wants. This is part of the technical side of music, and another reason why the appreciation of music must be both mental and emotional. Each instrument has its own character, and affects the emotions and the mind in its own individualistic way. There are even specific thoughtforms associated with individual instruments and the composer must consider all this when he is writing music. He doesn't consider it consciously, of course; it is part of his intuitive grasp of music. But the choice is really quite complex, depending on the kind of effect you want to create.

Both Western and Eastern music have rich traditions which help guide the composer in making these choices, but there is also an inner or esoteric side to the issue, as you correctly suggest. And that is a definite factor to keep in mind in selecting music either to heal or to enrich consciousness.

I don't think this is the time or the place to go into a lengthy exploration of the esoteric impact of each instrument, but it is a fascinating subject, and I hope someone picks it up and makes a study of it.

Leichtman: Yes. Well, let me ask you about the responsibility of musicians for contributing to a good performance. You made some comments earlier about the professionalism of musicians. Can you add anything else about what they should do or avoid to be most effective?

Wagner: Well, as I suggested earlier, the most critical element is the right attitude. I am assuming, of course, that we are talking about professional musicians who are technically competent in playing their instruments and who have adequately rehearsed the piece they are playing. The need for that kind of preparation is obvious. But beyond that, musicians need to realize that it is very difficult to give a good performance if they walk into the concert hall in an ugly mood or feeling angry toward someone. They need to learn to leave their problems at the door of the concert hall, so that their emotions will be relatively calm and be able to respond to the music. To my mind, this kind of psychological self-control is an essential part of a musician's professional skills.

The ability to admire and love whatever work is

being performed greatly enhances the quality of the performance. If a musician tries to play a piece when he is in an ugly mood, however, it will interfere with the beauty and brilliance inherent in the piece. His technical performance may still be satisfactory, but his attitude does not match the intent of the music. He is sending out ugly thoughts and feelings to the audience—and keep in mind what we said earlier. The audience is highly vulnerable to the projections of the musicians.

Leichtman: Can you go into any greater detail about what is actually happening in such cases?

Wagner: Well, as you know, anger, fear, sadness, and the other negative emotions trap you in a low level of the emotional plane. But in addition to that, they are insidiously destructive to any effort to be refined, brilliant, or inspired. Now suppose a musician who is trapped in a negative emotion is to play a heroic passage—something from one of my operas, or something from Beethoven or Franck or Rachmaninoff or someone else—which is designed to lift the audience into a quietly ecstatic state of rhapsodic thought and feeling. A musician who was angry or depressed would be totally out of harmony with the intent of this piece—or to put it in terms more customary for a musician, he would be out of touch with the real music and beauty of the piece. And that would make it almost impossible for him to play this music in such a way that he could communicate the intended effect to the audience. From my perspective, that is almost an unforgivable sin—especially if he happened to be playing my material!

[Laughter.]

The comments we made earlier about the need of the

listener to appreciate both the technical, intellectual and the emotional, beautiful sides of music are even more relevant to the musician. He must be very keenly aware of the beauty and inner quality of the music he is playing, and participate in creating an atmosphere in which this beauty can develop fully, in addition to playing the piece well from a technical standpoint.

Leichtman: How does the musician know how to create a proper emotional atmosphere or feeling of beauty for a piece of music, or even for the different passages within a single piece?

Wagner: The music itself contains the inspiration which will guide the musician into the correct attitude, as long as he is responsive to it and willing to let it move his thinking and feeling. With practice, a professional musician should be able to do this with no problem—because he is a human being, not an instrument without feelings!

This can be a spiritual experience for the musician, and in many cases, it is. I might even say it should be, and *will* be, if the musician will approach the playing of the music with reverence and adoration. There is a time and place for the technical work of study, study, study and practice, practice, practice. But by the time of the actual performance before an audience, the technical side should be mastered. By that point, the focus should have shifted to communing with the beauty and power of the music. It is the capacity of the musician to do this—to approach the music with the right attitude—which makes the difference between a technically correct but dull performance and a brilliant performance. The musician must *enjoy* performing, *enjoy* playing the music, and let the music lift him to the heights which inspired the composer.

Leichtman: I understand. I remember attending a concert performed by an orchestra on tour. They were playing ten cities in twenty-one days or something like that—the kind of thing we can do nowadays with airplanes. It was obvious that the orchestra members were tired and uncomfortable. They played some lovely pieces, but the total effect, at least to my ear, was somewhat marred by a lack of brilliance and sensitivity to the music.

Wagner: Absolutely. Of course, we didn't have jet lag in my day, but in many ways travel was even more fatiguing. It is important not to schedule performances too closely.

Leichtman: Let me change the subject and talk about conductors. What is the responsibility the conductor bears in bringing out the best of the music and the orchestra's performance?

Wagner: A lot of people wonder what a conductor does—I know many musicians ask themselves that question! *[Laughter.]* Actually, conducting is a complex and difficult task when performed correctly, especially in opera. Some of the responsibilities of the conductor are obvious, of course—getting everyone started on the same beat and finishing on the same beat—but the conductor must also take the reins of the whole production, and in opera, that can become most complex. Not every musician has the skill to do it well. It is a real challenge of leadership.

The conductor, for example, must determine how strong each section of the orchestra should be in a particular piece—and that can affect the effect the music has. If there are soloists or singers performing with the orchestra, he must adjust the whole orchestra to them. There are some conductors, of course, who imperiously demand that the soloists adjust to the orchestra, but this is usually not fair or correct.

I hope you appreciate that I am taking a broader view of some of these issues than I would have as a conductor when I was alive physically.

Leichtman: Yes, you were known to be somewhat imperious yourself.

Wagner: I was very passionate about my music. As a rule, everyone involved in a performance—the conductor, the musicians, and the soloists—should adapt themselves to the way the composer intended the music to sound. If the conductor happens to be the composer himself, he may well start to behave imperiously! Even if he is not, however, it is part of his role to determine the intent of the composer and to lead the orchestra in adhering to it. But one of the major rules of music is that you must not enforce your ideas or interpretations so strictly that you crush the spirit of the music. There is a human element to performing music that must be taken into account—because it is this human element which gives the performance life and vigor.

Leichtman: Yes, I have heard well-known soloists complain that certain conductors all but ignore them except during the actual performance. It injects an element of competition and antagonism which dishonors the spirit of the music and jeopardizes the performance.

Wagner: Exactly. And in opera, these issues become much more complex, because you have more soloists to deal with, and all of the problems of creating both a stage play and a symphony. They have to be coordinated so that each enhances the other. If you don't have a good conductor, the result will be chaos.

Leichtman: My psychic perception is that sometimes the conductor serves as a divine magician or theurge who pulls in the inspiration and evokes masterful performances from all of the musicians, somehow knitting it all together.

Wagner: I would rather think of the composer as the divine magician, and the conductor as his assistant. The conductor should think of himself as working hand in hand with the composer—even if the composer has gone on to the other world.

Leichtman: What do you mean by that?

Wagner: Exactly what I said. A good conductor should speculate on what moved and inspired the composer, what motivated him to write the score as he did, what effect he was striving to create, and so on. The good conductor should stretch his professional knowledge and imagination so as to almost reach out and tap the composer's genius. That would be the basis for an outstanding performance.

Japikse: How much leeway does the conductor have in interpreting the music?

Wagner: As much as the music itself permits. If a conductor tries to impose his own personal style on a piece of music, he may find the music itself will tend to correct him. But if he tries to tap the essence of the music and let it guide him, he may be surprised how much leeway there really is.

I must confess that I was most exacting about performances of my work—perhaps too much so. But then I thought of my operas as my own creations, and like a proud parent, I wanted my children treated with exquisite care. I think the results I achieved justified the fuss I made over so many of the details.

What I understand better now is that the inspiration for classical music is not engraved in marble. An individual or group may try to freeze a piece of music in marble, but inspiration does not originate in that kind of rigidity. A good performer should strive to recapture the original inspiration that moved the composer and then add to it from his own genius. With a symphony or the opera, the conductor should try to do the same. When this happens, the result is likely to be an inspired performance.

Now, this is not to say that there are unlimited variations on the original inspiration, but it is surprising how much latitude there actually is.

Leichtman: How would a musician or a conductor invoke this kind of inspiration and tap the conscious intent of the composer? I am sure many people would claim this is not possible.

Wagner: It may be difficult for some people, but it is certainly not impossible. Inspiration, when it is first perceived, does seem to be so spontaneous and fleeting that I can understand why many people would believe it to be impossible to recreate it for every performance. It seems to be less tangible than a breeze. But I for one can authoritatively state that it *is* possible to recapture the state of mind and emotion in which the composer first experienced the insight and sense of beauty which became the basis for his composition. The thrill and power may not be as strong as it was originally, but the essence remains.

In fact, this is precisely what good music is designed to do—to lift you up to heaven for a moment to share a portion of the music. This is the ennobling work of music and its potential benefit for all of us. It can lift us beyond ordinary states of feeling and thinking to a more transcendent level. But if the conductor or the musician isn't able to reach these transcendent levels, how can he expect his audience to be lifted up?

Leichtman: Along this same line of thought, I know that Roberto Assagioli, the founder of Psychosynthesis, has recommended listening to passages of *Parsifal* as a means of helping people reach the higher self, and for promoting integration of the spirit and the personality.

Wagner: That's exactly what I had hoped for when I wrote that. I don't mean to imply that I envisioned psychotherapists recommending my music as a twentieth century ladder to heaven, but I did hope that people would be deeply moved and uplifted by hearing my operas, and inspired by the same qualities and forces that I was inspired by.

Leichtman: We've already mentioned Corinne Heline. She wrote many books on the esoteric effect of music, especially your music *[The Esoteric Music of Richard Wagner]*. She explores rather extensively the potential of your music to help an individual contact the higher self, and describes how the musical forms take shape in the aura of the listener. She was quite clairvoyant and describes this from her own clairvoyant observations.

Wagner: Yes, I am familiar with her works. They are quite valid, especially when she writes about the intent and effect of classical music.

Japikse: And it is the role of the conductor to convey something of this potential or richness of the music to the musicians?

Wagner: Yes. Of course, there are some practical

limits to how far a conductor can go. If he starts talking about integrating the personality with the higher self, he might be considered weird. *[Laughter.]* The best way a conductor can communicate his understanding of the inner essence of a piece of music is through his reverence for it and his patient handling of the work. That would be a sign that some degree of the original inspiration is moving through him.

Leichtman: I'm not sure that "patience" is the right word for all conductors. I remember watching Toscanini rehearsing an orchestra. He seemed to drive individual members of the orchestra absolutely to a frenzy and to the limits of their creative capacity. He left them exhausted—some angry, some in shock. Yet he pulled a magnificent performance out of them.

Wagner: That was his personal technique for whipping up respect for the score they were performing, and for him it worked. I suspect it was also a matter of his Italian nature.

Leichtman: Okay. Well, let's move on then to the role of the composer. What special responsibilities does the composer have?

Wagner: It would depend on the purpose of the music he is writing. If he seeks merely to entertain or to thrill, then the composer has a limited responsibility. Some of the modern scores for movies, for example, are designed chiefly to entertain and to enhance the mood of the movie at appropriate points. I am actually aware of a good deal of this music, and I approve of most of it. It may be the only contact with good music that the majority of people will ever have. In most cases, the music which accompanies movies has only a limited scope and potential, but many brilliant gems are hidden away here and there.

Leichtman: Yes, Vaughn William's seventh symphony was composed for the movie about Scott's ill-fated adventures at the South Pole, but it has great power and majesty. And Sir William Walton's score for the movie *Richard the Third* is also memorable.

Wagner: Many of these compositions are extensions of the tone poem—a statement which may offend some critics, even though it's a fact. Given the limited purpose much of this music is meant to serve, I think many of these composers have done brilliant work and deserve much credit.

But obviously I am holding these compositions to a different standard than the usual fare for symphony halls. Writing what I will call the traditional classical music is a complex art, whether you look at it from my current perspective or from yours.

I think if I'm going to discuss the role of the composer, I'd better divide my comments into three categories—how the composer serves the overall purpose of classical music, the creative process of composing the score, and the schools of music. I will be discussing these subjects from my current perspective, not necessarily from the perspective I held during my lifetime as Richard Wagner. Also keep in mind that while the points I make are quite true, the composer in a physical personality may not be aware of all of them consciously. Some of these things operate at unconscious levels, and affect the composer automatically, without his conscious awareness of them. I don't want to leave the impression that great composers literally think in these ways.

I will first address the purpose the composer serves.

Simply stated, the composer must align himself with the purpose of music itself and give it a passageway for birth into the physical plane. To serve this purpose, the composer must prepare himself or herself with a vast knowledge and experience in the technical side of music. He or she must also bring into the creative work an enormous talent and a great sense of beauty. These last two items are qualities you must be born with—they cannot be acquired in a one-semester college course!

Now, assuming that the composer has this necessary talent, sense of beauty, and technical knowledge and expertise, what else must he have to become a great composer? As I have already suggested, he must also have a deep respect and love for music—a passion for music which rivals the intensity of religious adoration. He must view music as one of the languages of God and see himself as a musical prophet who reveals the beauty and inspiration of God to those who have the ears to hear. The dedication of the person who intends to write great music must approach a level of being intoxicated with the divine. For when he is, then inspiration pours forth and the composer is impelled to create with a majesty he could never summon through his personal resources.

These statements may be considered flamboyant and grandiose by some, but this is the way I approached writing music, and I devoutly believe the same principles are valid for others. No doubt other composers would define the purpose of music differently, but the same dedication and attitude must be there to set the talent and the sense of beauty into action.

Leichtman: That's very impressive. You make composing great music sound as though it were a divine mission.

Wagner: It is! Music is meant to inspire the audience as it originally inspired the composer. Great music is designed to stimulate the seeds of spiritual perfection on earth, especially in the human mind and emotions. And because music can speak directly to the subconscious and the unconscious, its message and inspiration can be very powerful and effective. This is an awesome responsibility for the composer to bear.

Leichtman: Just how effective is music in inspiring the public and changing their consciousness?

Wagner: It would be very difficult for sociologists to quantify it, if that's what you mean, because the effect is on the subconscious and unconscious mind. It is not immediately apparent. It couldn't be measured by opinion polls. But we were talking earlier about studies on the harmful effects of rock and roll music, and I am being told now, by someone up here, about some other studies that have been conducted where students were exposed to silence, classical music, and rock and roll music. Following this exposure, their behavior, intellectual skills, and muscular coordination were tested, and the results showed that good classical music produced an improvement in all three categories over silence, while rock and roll music caused a deterioration.

Leichtman: But what about proof of the long range beneficial effect of classical music?

Wagner: I'm afraid there is none that will satisfy a modern scientist. But if short-term beneficial effects can be documented, just think what frequent and long-term exposure to classical music can do.

Let me say this. If you can accept the idea that classical music promotes the themes of compassion, sympathy, refinement, nobility, optimism, and kindness, then there is bound to be a wholesome effect which stimulates maturity and enlightenment in general. If it can lift up the mind and heart of individual music lovers, then it can also have a similar impact on the masses over a long period of time.

Leichtman: Is the impact guaranteed to be favorable, even if the music is lofty? There are critics, as I'm sure you know, who associate you with Hitler's ambition and aspirations. Do you think your music contributed in any way to the rise of the Nazis?

Wagner: Actually, I'm glad you asked that question, as I would like to make a statement clearing up this bit of nonsense. First of all, I resent being held guilty of anything by mere association. If Mussolini liked Puccini, that should not in any way detract from the value and beauty of Puccini's music, should it?

Hitler was an extremely talented propagandist. He knew how to appeal to the masses, and one of the first rules of any demagogue is to wrap yourself in the traditions of your country and hide behind its heroes. It is a clever way of disguising your devious intentions and to cover up your flaws. Well, Hitler hid behind some of my music for that reason.

My operas are centered around the life of a hero who is deliberately made to seem larger than life because he is supposed to represent the struggles and aspirations of the traveler on the spiritual path—or at least a noble quest of some kind. This hero is motivated by a strong sense of destiny, and often must endure terrible tests or punishments. Grand opera is like that, and I squeezed every drop of sweat, blood, and tears out of my characters. But these are themes which do, unfortunately, appeal to egomaniacs of every kind, as well as people of noble attitudes and convictions. This is unfortunate, but hardly a reason not to use those elements in opera. Hitler's ambition and ferocious greed were fed by his own malicious mania, *not my operas!* I *refuse* to take any blame for what he did!

And keep in mind that any significant creative work can be misused. The best example of that would be the Christian scriptures. Smallminded people have used them time and time again to malign and curse others or to stir up guilt and fear, yet that was clearly not the intention of Jesus or His disciples.

Leichtman: No, indeed. I think you answered your critics very well.

Should we move on to the creative process of the composer?

Wagner: The main thing to say about this is that the composer must prepare for inspiration and learn to keep his channels open for these impulses of creativity. You can't learn inspiration from a book or a course, but you can prepare your thinking and values so that inspiration can come to you and keep on coming.

Leichtman: Can you be more specific?

Wagner: Sure. I'm not really talking here about developing a basic competence in composition. That is such a basic requirement that it goes without saying. I'm talking here about the special preparation the composer must make in order to invoke inspiration. And this is done by carefully preparing your mind with a vision of what you hope to create. This could be a general philosophy on life, a sense of heroic destiny, a new insight into the laws of harmonics, or a reverence for the national spirit of the country in which the composer dwells. It would be different for each individual. But it must be a carefully constructed vision or set of values that will give focus to the creative process. This kind of structure is extremely useful in organizing the creative process. Until I developed one, my creations were not worth very much.

Leichtman: Yes, I heard a recording of one of your earliest compositions. It sounded as though I was being fired at by one hundred machine guns. Personally, I couldn't stand it. I understand you were fired by the city that had hired you after that piece was performed.

Wagner: Well, we all make our little mistakes while we are trying to find our correct place in the scheme of things. But you are right—it was awful, and I am sorry that history even saw fit to record a performance in modern times.

To return to what I was saying earlier, I did not create any of my outstanding work until I focused on the theme of heroism and the emerging nobility of our humanity.

Japikse: Some of your critics have suggested that you merely borrowed prevalent myths of the German people and added your music to them.

Wagner: But that doesn't make it any less creative. Yes, I made much use of the myths of the culture I grew up in, but they were just old stories until I turned them into grand opera! Frankly, I decided that stories about heroes and heroines would present my ideas better than some dreary plot about a housewife in Berlin who was disappointed by a boring husband and titillated by a dashing prince in disguise. *[Laughter.]* I was interested in the dignity of mankind, and I thought that these legendary stories presented this theme better than anything I might make up.

Japikse: Excuse me—I didn't mean to imply that you were taking short cuts in creativity. I think you took the old myths and greatly enriched them, and even promoted a greater awareness of the rich tradition of myths in your culture.

Wagner: Why, thank you. It was a two-way street. The myths enriched my work, and I think I enriched them in return. I certainly did give them new visibility, as you suggested. Who would know about Siegfried, after all, if I hadn't written that opera?

Japikse: Yes. Unfortunately, a lot of modern people seem to think that mythology is by nature false, but it is not. It is something which should be a very important part of our life, as much of our culture is embodied in myths.

Wagner: That's right. Mythology is not trivial at all; it captures the greatness of life. Mythology is meant to be a way we learn about and relate to the heroism and nobility in people, our nation, the values of our culture, and so on. The ancient Greeks and Egyptians and many other cultures drew on their myths to create marvelous plays and pageants. The role of mythology is to help us know who we are and what we are able to do culturally, and to convey these ideas on to the masses, thereby keeping the culture fresh and alive with great ideas and themes.

All of this, you see, makes the story larger than life to the beholder, and that makes for good theater. Maybe I should say, "It makes for great theater." *The Marriage of Figaro* makes for good theater. It is a marvelous opera, but it is basically intended to be a romp. It presents nothing larger than life. It is a masterpiece of its kind, but the characters are just ordinary people in common human situations, somewhat transcended by the musical environment they are presented in.

But to my mind, great theater presents a picture that is larger than life. So I used mythology.

There's another reason why I chose to use mythology, too. I wanted to do pieces which would deal with human suffering and human tragedy. But I didn't really want to depress everyone in the audience. So I made it a towering kind of tragedy and suffering, ten times greater than anyone would ever suffer in real life, so I could examine the tragedy and expound on it. That's where the myths are so useful. I could build up a tragedy of such gigantic proportions that it didn't add any sense of tragedy, any heavy burden, to the audience. I made the suffering the type that only a demigod would experience, rather than something the audience would identify with directly.

That let me examine tragedy as a force of life in such a way that the audience could identify with the symbolic theme of struggle.

Leichtman: Yes, and you had a marvelous way of bringing in the divine presence in these cosmic struggles. It is not always blatantly obvious, but more like Rembrandt seeking to reveal the inner and noble qualities in ordinary people. You were also quite masterful in bringing out the redemptive power of divine force in the midst of tragedy and struggle.

Wagner: I like your interpretation. You should have been a music critic during my lifetime. Where were you when I needed you? *[Laughter.]*

Leichtman: Or where was I when Rembrandt needed me? *[More laughter.]* I think the comparison is merited. Of course, your themes are more obviously cosmic and universal. Rembrandt's treatment of those themes was perhaps more individual and personal. But there is great similarity.

Wagner: Yes, and I have been severely criticized because of that, as you know. There are some who object that my operas seem to be acted out by singing statues, not humans. But I wanted that monumental quality in my operas.

Japikse: That's not your deficiency—it's a deficiency among critics. There seems to be a whole class of them these days who have no appreciation for mythology at all. If a play or opera or movie doesn't deal with "real people," they dismiss it as irrelevant.

Wagner: You have them in your time, too? How about that! *[Laughter.]*

Well, this brings up another point about the responsibility of the composer, and that is to understand the need of every creative person to preserve his own values and dignity. We have already talked a little about this subject when you asked me about criticism earlier, but I want to expand somewhat on what I've already said. The person who strives to stand apart from the rest of humanity is going to be criticized just because he is, indeed, standing apart. The creative person must accept this and adjust to it—otherwise, he will not be able to function. Some people are going to bitterly resent the fact that you are standing apart from the herd. To them, it is a form of rebellion. You are standing apart from the mainstream of humanity and saying, "I am not going to let you determine how I will live my life. I intend to determine that for myself.''

Leichtman: I would define a rebel as someone who puts his dominant effort into opposing something—not just in being different. You didn't so much attack the status quo as you promoted your own ideas. There is a difference there in both motive and result, even though it often appears to be the same thing to the less discerning eye.

Japikse: It seems to me that the major difference is between being innovative and being destructive.

Wagner: Well, I think I did effectively attack the status quo, at least in the area of music. Sometimes when you create you also attack the status quo by default—even when it is not your intent to be destructive. In any event, you can upset a lot of people just by being different!

Leichtman: Yes, I think we both know what you mean.

Your third category dealing with the responsibilities of the composer had to do with schools of music. Do you want to go on to that now?

Wagner: All right. It is well known that there are certain schools of music, just as there are certain schools of art—traditions of style, technique, and content which the individual composer or artist seeks to be guided by and add to. These traditions can be invaluable in helping a composer build up the vision and structure of values which are so very important in connecting him with inspiration.

What is not commonly known, however, is that the real schools of music are here on the inner planes, and the traditions of music are never broken, even though a school may come and go on the physical plane. The schools of music which emerge on the physical plane should be thought of as manifestations of these inner plane schools, and the great composers of each tradition as their representatives.

Now, there are many, many rich implications in this for the composer. As a young composer develops more and more expertise in the art of composing music, he will attract more and more assistance from the inner plane school of music he is associated with. From the composer's point of view, his connection with the inner school becomes a rich source of inspiration. From the point of view of the inner school, this working arrangement makes it possible to develop various long-range projects through an evolving succession of individual composers.

Now keep in mind that a composer in physical incarnation would probably not consciously know about his connection with the inner school. He would explain it some other way.

Leichtman: Of course. But there is certainly a great deal of evidence even on the physical level to support this idea. Certainly the works of Richard Strauss seem to have much in common with yours—and Brahms with Beethoven, Ravel with Debussy, and so on.

Wagner: There is a natural creative affinity which develops among certain composers, and this affinity can definitely be traced back to an association at the inner levels.

Leichtman: I can add that I can remember attending actual concerts on the inner planes—concerts that were very well attended.

Wagner: It's a regular part of our life on the inner

planes. Music was important and enjoyable to us during physical life, and it continues to be important in the life of spirit.

Leichtman: Am I right in assuming that the concerts I attended while out of the body were a part of these inner schools?

Wagner: Of course. Now, I want to make sure our readers don't get the wrong impression. I am using the term "school of music" in the sense of a musical tradition, rather than in the sense of a formal academy with strict entrance requirements and enforced attendance. This is a common use of the term, but one not everyone reading this interview may be familiar with.

The schools of music on the inner planes are formed by common interest and expertise. They develop long range plans for the evolution of music and its role in civilization and humanity. They enjoy music together. And they help one another and their agents in the physical plane.

Some of their sessions are attended by physical people during the time when their bodies are sleeping. These would usually be musicians or people with a deep interest in music. Most of the time, they would not remember having attended these sessions, but they might awaken with a fleeting memory of being at a concert or an opera. But even though they do not recall a concrete memory, they are enriched by an abstract memory which fortifies their own genius—a progressively greater measure of knowledge and insight about what to do in their creative work.

Leichtman: I presume this kind of contact with the inner plane schools would be an invaluable aid to the composer, both in producing new works and in evolving a richer perspective.

Wagner: Sure, but the real benefit of this contact is that it enlarges and magnifies the force of the inner team which works to inspire and guide the composer. I don't want to leave the impression that the contact is established primarily for the benefit of the development of the composer. The unfoldment of individual talent is more the responsibility of the composer's own genius.

Leichtman: Well then, what can an aspiring composer do to make this contact if he doesn't have it already?

Wagner: Nothing. The contact is made on the inner side, not by the personality wanting it.

Indirectly, of course, anything which would increase a composer's ability to serve as a representative of an inner school of music would help make the contact—increasing skill and competence, increasing dedication and devotion to the ideals of a particular school, and so on. A composer who was nothing but an unimaginative plodder who could only rephrase the brilliance of other composers would not attract much attention. But someone who was proving he could turn out good, solid work would. Common sense rules these issues, not esoteric knowledge or some exotic trick.

Leichtman: What about the English lady, Rosemary Brown, who says she is in contact with various "dead" composers who come to her and dictate pieces?

Wagner: What she claims is happening *is* happening.

Leichtman: But why is this being done? Why work with her instead of a very gifted musician who might be able to work at a more complex and rewarding level?

Wagner: I presume that you are referring to the fact

that this lady does not have much formal musical education and could not follow a complex score on her own. Yet if you look into it, some of the music which has been dictated through her is not all that simple. It exceeds her own capacities.

The reason some composers have worked with her is not so much to set the music world on its ear with magnificent new compositions as it is to demonstrate that we are still alive and creating. In addition, we are also demonstrating something about the process of inspiration—and doing it in a rather dramatic way. The poor lady has attracted a lot of unpleasant criticism in order to do this, and there are many people here who are grateful for her cooperation in this endeavor.

I should add that anyone who has heard her play and had the opportunity to talk with her a while can recognize that she does not have a sophisticated knowledge of music nor the skill to write these things herself. Of course, diehard skeptics will never agree with that judgment, but it is still true, nevertheless.

Yes, we much prefer to work with people who have done much to cultivate an expert knowledge of musical theory and the mechanics of composition, because they can register the inspiration in a more profound way. But that kind of person would probably be scared to death if a ghost walked up to him and he said he would like to dictate a new symphony to him. *[Laughter.]* And just dictating a whole piece to him would not be fair use of his talent, either.

The more complex and well prepared the mind of the composer is, the more sophisticated the transfer of insight and inspiration will be. In the case of a highly talented individual, it is far more likely that inspiration will occur at the level of direct mental impressions of the music itself, rather than a clairvoyant vision or some kind of automatic writing, which take place on the astral plane. The simpler, astrally-focused psychic apparatus is not as useful for transmitting abstract or complex themes and ideas.

Leichtman: I understand, but that is a statement which will upset certain people who believe psychic visions and voices are the very highest kind of inspiration possible.

Wagner: The truly great composer must strive to reach the very spirit of music, and tap its essence. This is the richest possible source of inspiration—and it is several octaves higher than the astral ability to see auras and discarnate spooks.

This is not to say that inspired geniuses never have clairvoyant glimpses or visions of their work, because they do. I certainly did. But these glimpses are not a primary channel for their creative inspiration.

Leichtman: Okay. Let me ask another question about the schools of music. What would be the esoteric purpose of the different schools?

Wagner: Let me begin by saying that these various schools are not all that separate. We are not in any way competing with one another for awards and plaudits. We are loyal to the spirit of music, not to finite theories and practices. The kind of loyalties and partisanship which is common at the physical level tends to fade away after we come over to this side. Partisanship is a phenomenon of the personality. To some degree, it helps keep the personality focused, but it would only interfere with the work we're trying to do here.

To understand the esoteric purpose of the schools of

music, you have to appreciate the fact that there are many different kinds of effects music creates. Chamber music promotes a refinement of taste and sensitivity. Impressionistic music stimulates a capacity to step beyond what our senses tell us and respond to an overall feeling or mental abstraction of what something means. It lifts consciousness out of the physical and obvious elements of life. Symphonies and concertos afford the opportunity to integrate various themes in complex ways and not just lift the listener out of himself but actually introduce him to a marvelous inner world of beauty and joy. A tone poem can capture the inner character—or perhaps the inner struggle—of a person, a group, or even an aspect of nature. They are marvelous mood pieces.

All of these different styles have their own particular charm, and can be enjoyed purely at face value, as respite from the harsh realities of the mundane world. But they also have the capacity to educate us to be more attentive to the inner worlds and to stimulate our imaginations—to help us learn that not all ideas and emotions arise out of physical life, but in fact there is a rich inner world waiting to be explored, an inner dimension of inspiration that music can lead us to.

All of the inner schools of music serve the basic ideal of using music to help lead people to this rich inner world. But naturally, just as physical people have different tastes in music, different areas of specialization arise at the inner levels. One school will specialize in developing and enriching a certain effect or potential in music, while another one will focus its efforts elsewhere. But the goal is the same.

Now, I don't want to leave the impression that composers are all arcane teachers in disguise, blasting spiritual themes and enlightenment into mass consciousness. We are musicians, not psychologists. Much of what we do is motivated solely by a love for the music itself. And we give priority to enriching the traditions of music and helping it to evolve along its destined course. But we are aware of the inner potentials of music. A flower has its perfume, and music has its beauty. Both perfume and beauty are invisible to most people, but here on the inner side of life, beauty is tangible. And we know this beauty has a direct relationship with human attitudes and thinking. And so we try to develop the power of music to aid in the healing of mind and body, the enrichment of mass consciousness, and the work of bringing new spiritual light into the physical realm.

That is the esoteric purpose of the inner schools of music.

Leichtman: That's a very rich description of a powerful aspect of all art.

Wagner: Well, the real power of culture is not widely appreciated.

Japikse: Let me ask this question. How do you think your own work has been presented in modern times?

Wagner: For the most part, I am quite pleased. I am naturally gratified that they continue to be performed, and that many people have recognized the more profound elements within them. The operas are often performed a bit differently than I would have staged them, but they are open to interpretation, after all, and of course, the technology of staging an operatic production is now very much improved.

Japikse: We've already talked about the fact that your operas are designed to stimulate the heroic elements in mankind. Do you see them as having that kind of impact on our culture today?

Wagner: There's no question that many, many people have been influenced in these ways by attending performances of my operas. It's hard to quantify the impact my work has had, but there is no question that the vast majority of people *need* to be stimulated to aspire to the best they are capable of and to involve themselves in noble causes. I am glad that my work plays a part in stimulating these changes.

Japikse: Well, I have the impression that during your lifetime you held a much more definite view that your operas were going to have a very dramatic impact on the whole of culture. Have you been satisfied with the response which has occurred?

Wagner: I am as pleased as I could reasonably expect to be. Keep in mind that I was somewhat intoxicated with my own work. As I said earlier, I was seeing it from the inside, and was fervently dedicated to its purpose. Like many people who have a busy life and enjoy a measure of public success, I may have seen it as something a bit larger than it actually was. Just as my heroes were always larger than life, and not some impoverished street singer or lovesick count, my aspirations and expectations were perhaps slightly larger than justified.

However, I do think I helped set a new high water mark for grand opera itself, and have been an inspiration for others. No, my work did not have the revolutionary impact on the performing arts that I predicted it would, but let me hastily add that it would have been wrong for one person's approach to the arts to have become as dominant as I envisioned, because that would mean that a great many artists and their works would have been either ignored or never produced.

So I am pleased with the general outcome of my work.

Leichtman: What would you have written if you had lived longer in the physical?

Wagner: More operas. *[Laughter.]* I probably would have written one that would have extended the theme of Parsifal. But this is irrelevant now. I would have kept on writing as long as I might have lived, that is for sure. The source of inspiration had not dried up for me—it never dries up for anyone who is competent and dedicated to the arts.

Leichtman: Yes. Well, we talked earlier about the different effect of instruments; let me ask you another question about instruments now. Why is it that older instruments are often favored over newer instruments—especially in the area of violins, cellos, and other stringed instruments? Is this just a tradition, or is there a reason for it?

Wagner: A musical instrument becomes impregnated with the vibrations of the beautiful music that has been played on it, and this alters the way the instrument plays, the tone it produces, and the ease with which it plays. Musicians usually love the music they play, and the instrument they play it on. All of this—their love, the musical vibrations, and talent with which they play—eventually saturates the instrument, transforming it from a dead object into a living instrument.

This is not just my personal fantasy—it is quite real. And from my current perspective, it is rather easy to tell when an instrument has been well used. It becomes something of a magical instrument.

Leichtman: Yes, I remember hearing a talk by a violinist who now plays with Paganini's violin. He was quite rhapsodic about its virtues and its effect on him.

Let me ask you about the somewhat controversial issue of musical transcriptions. Leopold Stokowski has done what I regard as wonderful work in transcribing parts of *Boris Godunov* [an opera by Modest Mussorgsky] into an orchestra piece. I have heard excerpts from your operas performed on the piano. And recently I heard a transcription done by Franz Liszt of Beethoven's sixth symphony for the piano. What do you think of transcriptions?

Wagner: For the most part, I don't approve of them. It is like someone coming in to repaint the Mona Lisa in a different style—with a modern hairstyle or a red dress. *[Laughter.]* We have to assume that the original composer chose the instruments, the manner of presentation, and the scoring for very good reasons—and probably put his whole genius into making those choices. To then change these elements to come up with a different effect is, in general, an insult to the composer who did the original work.

Now in some cases, the transcription was an effort to make the music more available and popular. Liszt, for example, was working in a time when there were no radios or recordings. It was unlikely that most people would ever hear the whole of Beethoven's sixth symphony more than a few times in their lives. So transcribing it for piano made it more available.

Leichtman: I understand. But I still think that what he did was rather like trying to transpose the art of the

Sistine Chapel on to a postage stamp. *[Laughter.]* Most of the majesty and beauty was lost, I'm afraid.

Wagner: I think even Liszt would agree that much was lost in the process, but he was actually trying to promote the music and make it more available to the public.

Leichtman: Can you tell us something about the future of music and where it is headed? I know the technical advances in instruments and electronically-generated sounds must open up new opportunities. What is going to happen?

Wagner: We are entering an era in which new sounds and a new style will be developed. It may stir up a rebellion among those who are devoted to the recent traditions, but it will be a new wave of evolution for classical music.

Leichtman: Do you mean we will have electric violins and harps?

Wagner: I guess that's possible, but I doubt if it will be necessary or desirable. No, I was referring in part to the emergence of new capacities to use electronically-created sounds—and complex instruments that are run like a computer.

Leichtman: Something like a Moog synthesizer?

Wagner: Yes. These devices, and future generations of these devices, will produce a new variety of sounds and patterns not previously available for composing in classical music.

Now, this will be a marvel for the composer, as he will be able to create on one instrument complex sounds that would ordinarily require a group of competent musicians to produce. This will enable him to experiment with different effects and produce a composition which can be performed nearly the way the final piece will sound. Likewise, with computers the scoring can be accomplished with great speed and with many variations, if desired. This will save an immense amount of time which can then be devoted to additional experimentation or composing.

Leichtman: I'm not sure I want to hear a new symphony dominated by electronic beeps and vibratos, though. I hope they don't abandon the piano, the violin, and the other traditional instruments too soon.

Wagner: There is no cause to worry about that. We would not want a symphony orchestra replaced by a computer, a tape, and amplifiers and speakers. That is not what I'm describing. What I am talking about is more like your word processor—using computers to help the composer accelerate the process of composing, and even experiment with new sounds and combinations of sounds that will be both revolutionary and exciting. In some cases, it will be possible to generate whole new effects not just in terms of physical sound but also in terms of the effect mentally and emotionally.

Leichtman: Well, how are orchestras going to create these new sounds if not on the keyboard of some computer gadget?

Wagner: That is a problem we are working on. It is important that we do not lose the inspiration and contribution of the individual musicians in the actual performance. They are very important in generating the beauty and life of music, both through their skills and their reverence for the music they are playing. But this problem will be solved in time. It will take some creativity, but it can be done.

Leichtman: Well, it sounds intriguing. I look forward to it.

Wagner: It has already begun here and there, but it really isn't being recognized yet as a part of the classical music tradition. Most people simply think of it as experimental music or a weird offshoot of rock. It isn't, but only time will prove that.

Leichtman: Well, let me ask this. What would you like to see done in the area of musical education of our school children?

Wagner: Young school children ought to be more commonly exposed to classical music than is presently the case in the school system. The public schools today do a fair job of teaching singing and the rudiments of playing an instrument in the school band, but they could do far more in teaching music appreciation. In particular, I would like to see them emphasize the humanizing and civilizing effect of art in general.

Leichtman: I would hope they would also indicate that barbaric tendencies in art and music tend to "decivilize" people, if I can use that term.

Wagner: Well, that might stir up more controversy than would be worthwhile. And it is a bit difficult to prove that it does, although you are absolutely correct. Anyway, if real music appreciation—as I outlined it earlier—were taught in the public schools, we wouldn't have to worry about the bad music so much. It would be discarded fairly quickly.

Leichtman: Do we have the teachers who could teach music appreciation in the way you defined it?

Wagner: Probably not, but this can be readily taught to anyone who innately likes good music. They just need to realize that what they experience in listening to good music is something more than "good vibes" or an electric excitement. It is a spiritual uplift, a sense of peace, a surge of joy—a communion with the inner essence of music and an invitation to explore the rich inner world of music. Many people know this intuitively, but they need to learn to verbalize it. If they learn that, they could teach music appreciation.

Leichtman: Very good. What, may I ask, are you doing now that you are in spirit—besides talking to us, that is?

Wagner: I'm actually working on this idea of the music doctor. Several of us are establishing some basic rules and types of music that can be used for various kinds of healing. And I am also working on a project to broadcast good music directly from the inner planes to earth, without relaying it through physical agents. As you know, the usual way of grounding higher energies and insights is to work with a group of responsive people who are physically incarnate. Well, we are experimenting to see how well we can use music to influence the physical plane without such agents.

Leichtman: How is it working?

Wagner: It is still too early to tell yet. It will take a while to measure the impact of this.

Leichtman: I may have tuned in to some of this work at times.

Wagner: I'm sure you have.

Leichtman: What is the goal of this invisible concert beamed at earth?

Wagner: We are trying to promote a mood which facilitates tolerance, brotherhood, kindness, and cooperation. This is the general theme we are working on; there are other aspects to it, too, but that should be enough to stimulate your imagination.

Leichtman: Well, I hope it is successful.

Wagner: Of course, we also tune into individual composers once in a while to see what they are doing and to give them a little assistance. My friends did that for me when I was working physically. We have groups here that work in these ways musically, just as there is a group of spirits that help you in your work.

Leichtman: Does this include attending rehearsals and concerts to give the conductor or the musicians a boost?

Wagner: Why sure. Every once in a while we will say, "Let's go back and remember what it was like," and we will zoom down and give someone the benefit of our presence and perspective. *[Laughter.]* It's fun—and usually rewarding for the people we work with.

Leichtman: I guess that's the bottom line—isn't it? Music ought to be fun, it ought to be enjoyable. Do you have any special comments on how you would like people to approach your music?

Wagner: I intended these operas to be a series of uplifting experiences. I tried to make each one a composition which would take the listener higher and higher into his own inner nature. And I guess that is the way I would suggest listening to them.

I tried to lure people into the music and then bash them with a large dose of inspiration.

Leichtman: It's more bash than lure, I think.

[Laughter.]

Wagner: Sometimes it worked and sometimes it didn't.

Leichtman: No, it *is* there. Sometimes when I'm exhausted, I will put on *Die Meistersinger,* and listening to it very much recharges me inwardly and outwardly.

Well, I think we've exhausted our questions. Do you have a closing statement you would like to make?

Wagner: I've said most of what I wish to say. Let me just stress the fact that music is an exceedingly complex art form capable of profoundly affecting humanity. It is far more than just a vehicle for amusement and entertainment; it is a language of God. And as a language of God, it can be used to heal and enrich the mind and the emotions, and to inspire people with noble ideals and qualities. There are many people who consider this idea absurd—I encountered them during my lifetime, and they are still around. But I am even more profoundly convinced that this is true now than before, and I am even more committed to helping in the process of enriching life through music.

I hope this interview will stimulate many people to think more deeply about the potential for music to stir up the greatness within them. I also hope some people will examine the potential harmful effects of bad music more carefully, and then do something constructive about it.

And for those who struggle to tap the inspiration to compose and perform music, let me assure you that there are vast forces of angels and spirits ready to assist you in fostering good work in music.

And on that note I will close. Thank you for this opportunity to speak.

Leichtman: Thank you for coming.

Japikse: Yes, and for bringing your inspiration with you.

Wagner: It was my pleasure.

GLOSSARY

ANGEL: An entity belonging to the angelic or devic kingdom. Angels are not discarnate humans and have never been humans—they are part of a separate kingdom of life and have their own function and evolution. Still, their work and interests do bring them in touch with humans quite frequently—although humans are often unaware of this contact, as angels are invisible to ordinary sight. The angelic kingdom includes nature spirits, angels, and archangels.

ARCHETYPE: A basic pattern or ideal of creation. Archetypes are found at the abstract levels of the mental plane and are used by the soul as it creates the personality, its destiny, and its behavior. They are also used by nonhuman intelligences (such as angels) in creating nonhuman forms and conditions.

ASTRAL PLANE: The plane of the emotions and desires. The astral plane is an inner world made of matter that is more subtle than physical substance, yet interpenetrates all physical substance.

AURA: The light observed by psychics around all life forms. It emanates from the surface and interior of the various subtle bodies connected with a physical body. Thus, it is possible to see the aura of the etheric body (the health aura), the astral body (the emotional aura), and the mental body (the intellectual aura).

AUTOMATIC WRITING: A form of writing in which the pen or typewriter is controlled by some entity or force other than the conscious mind of the writer. The controlling entity could be the subconscious of the writer, an elemental, a spirit, or the soul of the writer.

CLAIRVOYANCE: The capacity to see or know beyond the limits of the physical senses. There are many degrees of clairvoyance, allowing the clairvoyant to comprehend forces, beings, and objects of the inner worlds normally invisible to the average person.

CONSCIOUSNESS: The capacity to know and be aware. It must be distinguished from *sensation,* which is the perception of objects, feelings, events, or ideas through the five physical senses or their emotional and mental counterparts. *Consciousness* is the ability of a unit of intelligence to reason on, reflect about, and draw conclusions regarding the nature of any other unit of intelligence or manifestation—and also itself.

DARK NIGHT OF THE SOUL: A period of spiritual crisis, in which the awareness of the soul which has been previously attained is obscured, forcing the aspirant to go beyond it and discover new dimensions and treasures of the inner life.

DIMENSION: A measurement of size, space, movement, or consciousness. There can be dimensions of thought and feeling as well as physical dimensions.

ENLIGHTENMENT: Focused in the light of the inner life of spirit. An enlightened mind is one that is capable of directly contacting this inner life and using its light to perceive, comprehend, and apply the spirit's wisdom. An enlightened personality is one that is governed and directed by an enlightened mind, in tune with the wisdom and love of the spirit.

ESOTERIC: An adjective which refers to knowledge of the inner worlds and inner life. In this book, it is used to refer to the knowledge of spirit—and to the body of teachings known as the Ancient Wisdom.

EVOLUTION: The growth of any life form to its destined perfection. It is the response of consciousness to the divine impulse to grow.

FOURTH DIMENSION: A realm of existence in which there can be four different planes of movement from a single point, each of these planes being separated by ninety degrees. All physical solids are part of this larger, fourth-dimensional realm. The movement of a fourth-dimensional solid through the physical plane would be recognized as a change in the apparent three-dimensional shape of that object, such as in the growth of a tree. We act in fourth-dimensional ways every day—by associating relevant memories to current experience, by speculating about our future, and by perceiving underlying motives and attitudes of other people. Loosely speaking, the astral plane could be considered the fourth dimension.

GOD: The Creator of all that exists, visible and invisible; the life principle and creative intelligence underlying all life forms and phenomena.

HIGHER SELF: The animating principle in human consciousness—the inner being or soul. It is the guiding intelligence of the personality, the part of the human mind that is immortal.

INNER PLANES: A term used to refer to any one of several inner worlds or levels of existence, all of which interpenetrate the dense physical plane. Each physical human being exists on these inner planes as well as on the physical level, by dint of having bodies composed of matter drawn from them.

INVOCATION: The process of calling forth assistance or inspiration from the inner levels of life, either through prayer, ritual, or creative activity.

MAGIC: In its original sense, the acts of a Magus or wise person with conscious awareness of the inner life of spirit. Pure magic, therefore, is the focusing of creative energies for the transformation of forms. It brings heaven to earth and enriches the earth.

MANTRA: A word or phrase silently repeated for the purpose of calming our thoughts and feelings.

MASS CONSCIOUSNESS: Literally, the mind and emotions of the human race as a single whole. To some degree, the thinking and feeling of every human being contributes to mass consciousness and—to a much larger degree—is powerfully influenced and conditioned by mass consciousness.

MEDITATION: An act of mental rapport in which the ideals, purposes, and intents of the inner life are discerned, interpreted, and applied by the personality. To be meaningful, meditation must be a very active state in which creative ideas, new realizations, and inspirations are pursued with vigor. A thorough description of meditation can be found in the book *Active Meditation: The Western Tradition* by Robert R. Leichtman, M.D. and Carl Japikse.

MEDIUM: A person who practices mediumship, the phenomenon of a nonphysical intelligence, usually a discarnate human, assuming some degree of control of a physical body in order to communicate something meaningful and useful.

MYSTIC: One who loves, reveres, and *finds* God and His entire Creation.

MYTH: A symbolic story which explains some mystery of human nature—its origins, its purpose, or its destiny. The current belief that myths are by nature false is itself a falsehood. For a story to be considered a myth, it must reveal some important truth about life.

NATURE SPIRIT: A primitive life form found on the etheric or the astral planes and involved in the work of nurturing and nourishing the forms of nature.

PERSONALITY: The part of the human being used for manifestation in the earth plane. It is composed of a mind, a set of emotions, and a physical body, each containing conscious and subconscious functions. It is the child of the inner life and its experiences on earth.

PSYCHIC: A person who is able to perceive events and information without the use of the physical senses. The word is also used to refer to any event associated with the phenomena of parapsychology.

SPIRIT: In this book, a term used in three different ways: 1) to refer to the portion of a human being which survives death; 2) to describe the spiritual entity that guides the destiny of a nation and its culture; and 3) to refer to the highest immortal, divine essence within any life form.

SPOOK: An affectionate term for a discarnate.

SUBCONSCIOUS: The part of the personality not

being consciously used at any given moment. The subconscious is always active and greatly influences our conscious moods, thoughts, acts, and attitudes. It is psychically in tune with other portions of the inner planes—even if we are not consciously psychic.

SYMBOL: An image, thought, feeling, or event which contains a deeper significance than what is obvious from the outer form.

THEURGE: One who is able to invoke and use divine forces.

THOUGHTFORM: Literally, the form a thought takes on the plane on which it is created, usually the astral or mental. Visible only to clairvoyants, thoughtforms are nonetheless created by every human being during the ordinary processes of thinking and feeling.

TRANSCENDENT: Above the mundane levels of consciousness and self-expression. Many people falsely assume that the mere retreat into a state of psychological quietness is enough to achieve transcendence, but that is only a withdrawal from sensation. Transcendence is achieved by *focusing* our level of awareness in the life of spirit.

UNCONSCIOUS: The part of the mind not ordinarily accessible to the conscious mind. It is filled in part with repressed memories, desires, fears, and feelings. But there are other parts to the unconscious as well: the seeds of noble qualities, creative impulses, and memories of earlier lives.

VIBRATION: The movement of any energy particle, whether physical, astral, or mental in origin. The word is popularly used to refer to emanations of astral energy which are perceived by psychic sensitivity.

FROM HEAVEN TO EARTH

Both series of 12 interviews are available by subscription for $27 *each* (for foreign delivery, including Canada, $30), or $50 together ($55 for foreign delivery). Each interview is published as a paperback book.

The spirits interviewed in the first series of 12 are Edgar Cayce, William Shakespeare, Cheiro, Carl Jung and Sigmund Freud, C.W. Leadbeater, Sir Oliver Lodge, Thomas Jefferson, Arthur Ford, H.P. Blavatsky, Nikola Tesla, Eileen Garrett, and Stewart White. All 12 books are now in print.

The spirits interviewed in the second series of 12 are Albert Schweitzer, Rembrandt, Sir Winston Churchill, Paramahansa Yogananda, Mark Twain, Albert Einstein, Benjamin Franklin, Andrew Carnegie, Richard Wagner, Luther Burbank, and Abraham Lincoln. The final book will be an interview with a number of spirits, titled *The Destiny of America*. A new book is published every three months. The series will be completely in print by October 1983.

Orders can be placed by sending a check for the proper amount to Ariel Press, 2557 Wickliffe Road, Columbus, Ohio 43221-1899. Make checks payable to Ariel Press. Foreign checks should be payable in U.S. funds. In Ohio, please add 5½ % sales tax. *Be sure to specify which set of books you are purchasing (first or second series).*

Individual copies of the interviews are available at $3 plus $1 postage each. If 10 or more copies of *a single title* are ordered at one time, the price is $2 a book plus the actual costs of shipping.